THE AUSTRIAN ECONOMY
SINCE 1945

THE ROYAL INSTITUTE
OF INTERNATIONAL AFFAIRS

London : Chatham House, St James's Square, S.W.1
New York : 542 Fifth Avenue, New York 19

Toronto   Bombay
Melbourne   Wellington   Cape Town

OXFORD UNIVERSITY PRESS

THE
AUSTRIAN ECONOMY
SINCE 1945

by

K. W. ROTHSCIIILD

London & New York
ROYAL INSTITUTE
OF INTERNATIONAL AFFAIRS

First published 1950

PRINTED IN GREAT BRITAIN AT
THE UNIVERSITY PRESS
ABERDEEN

CONTENTS

FOREWORD

THIS short survey of the development of Austria's economy from the end of the Second World War until the time of devaluation in the autumn of 1949 was made possible by a grant from the University of Glasgow in the summer months of 1949. It tries to record in a short space the events of the four years which can be regarded as the immediate post-war transition period. It is true that in 1949 Austria was—even with her production surpassing pre-war levels—by no means 'back to normal'. A number of serious disequilibria still exist and are discussed in the concluding section. But these difficulties are likely to persist for some time, and cannot be regarded as a transitory post-war phenomenon. It seemed, therefore, justifiable to regard the period under review as a definite phase in Austria's post-war development, and it is hoped that this study will prove helpful to those interested in further developments in that country or in inter-country comparisons in post-war readjustment.

My thanks are due to Sir Hector Hetherington, Principal of the University of Glasgow, and Professor A. L. Macfie, Adam Smith Professor of Political Economy in the University of Glasgow, for making this study possible and for their continued kind interest; to Mr J. Cunnison, Director of the Department of Economic and Social Research in the University of Glasgow, for putting the facilities of his Department at my disposal; and to Dr F. Nemschak and Dr E. John, directors of the Austrian Institute for Economic Research, for granting me leave of absence while I was engaged in writing this study.

Professor A. L. Macfie has read through the whole manuscript and his suggestions have led to numerous valuable improvements. I also wish to thank Miss Hermia Oliver of the editorial department of Chatham House for the care taken in preparing the work for the press.

K. W. ROTHSCHILD

February 1950

I

THE PERIOD 1918-45

THE Austria that emerged in the spring of 1945 from seven years of German occupation found herself again facing serious economic problems just as at her first birthday after the First World War in 1918. But it would be a mistake to think that the problems of the first and second Republic are essentially the same. This is by no means so.

AUSTRIA BEFORE THE SECOND WORLD WAR

In 1918 the Austrian Republic was suddenly put on the map; the metropolitan province of a fifty-million empire turned into an independent country of seven million inhabitants. To the serious problems which thus arose from the necessary adjustment of a huge administrative and financial apparatus to the more limited needs of a smaller area were added the difficulties created by the protectionist policy of the States formerly incorporated in the Habsburg Empire,[1] which necessitated far-reaching changes in the country's economic and industrial structure and a new basis for its foreign trade relations. The difficulty of these readjustments and the failure to carry them out rapidly and energetically [2] constituted the main feature of the specific Austrian problem and the constant drag towards depression in the inter-war period.

While this problem was by no means completely solved

[1] A policy that was to a large extent justified by the former neglect of the industrial needs and potentialities of these regions.

[2] This failure, and the failure even to recognize the tasks to be achieved, were greatly helped by the inflow of foreign (mainly American) short-term credits in the nineteen-twenties which concealed the underlying difficulties. It was only when, under the influence of the world depression, these foreign credits were withdrawn that the full impact of the post-war situation was felt and the structure of the economy was readjusted.

For an account of the whole inter-war period see K. W. Rothschild, *Austria's Economic Development Between the Two Wars* (London, Muller, 1947). An interesting study of the development in the field of money and foreign exchanges in the nineteen-thirties is contained in Howard S. Ellis, ' Exchange Control in Austria and Hungary ', *The Quarterly Journal of Economics*, vol. 54, no. 1, pt. 2 (1940).

before the Second World War, the Austria of 1938 nevertheless represented an economic unit which had found a basis for developing an economic life of its own. Agriculture and the tourist traffic were greatly expanded, and new products and new markets were developed for the export trade so that the huge deficit in the balance of payments, which had been the main trouble in earlier years, could be wiped out. True, all this was achieved by strong deflationary methods which greatly restricted the volume of foreign trade and kept unemployment figures at a very high level—the number of registered unemployed was 321,000 in 1937, more or less a boom year in the rest of the world, compared with 192,000 in 1929 and 406,000 in 1933, the year with the worst unemployment record. Nevertheless, the foundations for an independent economic development were laid, and given a careful and more constructive economic policy the pre-war Austrian economy could have overcome these drawbacks. In short, a special Austrian problem ceased to exist.

THE EFFECTS OF THE ANSCHLUSS AND OF THE WAR YEARS

It will therefore be seen that the second Austrian Republic is not faced with the same problem of remodelling its economic life to meet a completely new situation as was the first one. While there can be no question of a simple return to the pre-Anschluss conditions of 1937, because too much has changed since then inside and outside of Austria, and because the 1937 position was anything but a balanced or satisfactory state of affairs, there exists nowadays at least a historical basis which in certain questions can act as a standard of reference, and which gives a much greater continuity to the country's economic development than was the case after 1918.

On the other hand, Austria is not merely a country changing over from war to peace conditions. For seven years her economy was completely absorbed into the German economy. During this period the Austrian economic structure was exposed to the double pressure of fitting into a war economy and of fitting into the needs of the German Reich. While some of these influences helped in the development of Austria's productive facilities they were not guided by the requirements of an independent Austrian peace-time economy. In no way did they continue the process of adjustment that had been going on in the nineteen-thirties, but on the contrary they added some new 'unbalances' to the situation.

When the Germans had invaded Austria their main aim in the economic field was to increase war production as fast as possible and to orientate the economic life of the country to a far greater extent towards Germany than had been the case before. The first aim was primarily achieved by a great expansion in the output of the heavy industries and in raw material production. The mining of iron ore increased from 1,885,000 tons [1] in 1937 [2] to 3,132,000 tons in 1943, and the production of oil, badly neglected in the pre-war years, rose steeply from 33,000 tons in 1937 to 1·2 million tons in 1944.[3] Against this there was a decline in the output of the light and consumer goods industries which had always played an important part in Austria's economy. The production of cotton yarn declined between 1937 and the first half of 1941 [4] by 47 per cent. Apart from the influx of foreign workers into the war industries there was a considerable shift of Austrian workers from peace-time to war-time occupations. An index of employment in 1,678 representative Austrian firms (mainly larger enterprises) compiled by the Viennese Arbeiterkammer (Chamber of Labour) shows that in March 1945 the total employment in these firms had increased to 239 (March 1934 = 100), but also that this change ranges from increases to 482 in the iron, steel and engineering industries and to 234 in the mines, to declines to 93 in distribution and to 85 in the textile industry.[5] If the smaller firms and the artisan

[1] Tons always refers to metric tons.

[2] 1937 was itself a good year in view of the rearmament demands of Italy, Germany, and Japan. In 1936 output had only been 85,000 tons, and in the depression year of 1933, 22,000 tons.

[3] These figures and the figures which follow later in the text and in the tables all come, if not otherwise stated, from the *Monatsberichte des Österreichischen Instituts für Wirtschaftsforschung*, published by the Austrian Institute for Economic Research, and from the *Statistische Nachrichten*, published by the Austrian Central Statistical Office. Detailed references have been omitted in order to avoid overloading the text with footnotes.

[4] This is the last war period for which data are obtainable. The figures for the first half-year of 1941 were adjusted for seasonal influence.

[5] There was already a slight trend towards the heavy industries in the years 1934-8. However, no index numbers are available for pre-war years except for the base year 1934.

enterprises were included in this survey the shift from the consumer goods industries would be far more marked. These shifts are, however, only one aspect of the problem. More important for the future, because more difficult to repair, is the fact that during the war years very few young people were apprenticed to a number of trades which in the past were of considerable importance for Austria's peace-time economy and exports.

INDEX OF EMPLOYMENT IN 1,678 AUSTRIAN
FIRMS IN MARCH 1945
(March 1934 = 100)

Mines	.	.	.	233·6	Clothing	.	.	115·2
Clay, glass, etc.	.	.	138·6	Paper	.	.	.	101·9
Building	.	.	215·4	Printing	.	.	.	102·9
Electricity	.	.	.	212·2	Chemicals	.	.	228·7
Iron, steel, engineering	.	481·8	Food	.	.	.	106·6
Timber	.	.	.	209·8	Hotels	.	.	.	121·0
Leather	.	.	.	140·3	Distribution	.	.	92·7
Textiles	.	.	.	84·7				

TOTAL (all firms) : 238·9

The fusion of the Austrian with the German economy was first of all carried out on the legal and administrative plane by the wholesale transfer of Austrian shares and other property rights into the hands of German industrial concerns, banks, and holding companies, a process that was greatly assisted by the widespread German permeation of Austria's economy that had existed long before the Anschluss.[1]

But in other fields, too, every attempt was made to orientate the Austrian economy towards Germany. In particular great efforts were made to shift the economic centre of gravity from the eastern parts of the country and from Vienna, which had been the traditional industrial regions and closest to the trade routes to the south and east of Europe, nearer to Germany, i.e. more to the west of the country. This desire determined to a large extent the location of the new enterprises that were built in order to increase the country's war potential. Later on, this 'trend towards the west' was intensified by strategic considerations, because the western provinces of Austria seemed safest from air attack.

In this way the period of the occupation led to an intensified

[1] Through direct ownership, control of shares, and numerous cartel agreements.

4

industrialization of the western parts of Austria, and particularly of the province of Upper Austria. In this province the German Government and German firms, together with Austrian firms, created a big Danube port at Linz (which later should have served Austro-German trade by a system of canals linking the Danube with German rivers) and three major enterprises: a big heavy industrial complex in Linz (originally part of the Hermann Goering concern), combining coke ovens, a steel mill and a nitrogen factory concentrating on the production of nitrate of lime and ammonia,[1] an important artificial fertilizer; the aluminium works in Ranshofen which had been planned to provide a large part of German-dominated Europe with aluminium; and the Zellwollefabrik (factory for wool made from artificial fibres) in Lenzing, which was attached to an existing paper and cellulose factory. Naturally, the establishment of these enterprises gave a considerable stimulus to new subsidiary industries and to industrial development in general. The end of the war and the first post-war period saw a further shift when some of the entrepreneurs transferred their assets to the west, partly because their Nazi record made them follow the retreat of the German army, partly because they expected socialization in the Russian-occupied zone. Since then there has been a certain return to the east, and the differential development in the different parts of Austria has come to an end. Nevertheless, the events of the previous years have left their mark. A census of the employed population taken by the Federal Ministry of Social Affairs in March 1948 showed that of those employed in industry and trade (excluding apprentices) 49·5 per cent were in the three eastern provinces (Vienna, Lower Austria, Burgenland) compared with 65 per cent in March 1934 when the last Austrian population census was taken.[2]

---

[1] The yearly capacity of the factory is 60,000 tons of nitrogen, which corresponds to 300,000 tons of nitrate of lime and ammonia. The latter represents about 90 per cent of the total value of output.

[2] It must, however, be remembered that this development has also been fostered by an uneven development in population growth. Vienna, with its considerable deficit in births, had always depended on migrants from the countryside to maintain and expand its population. This migration had decreased considerably during the war and first post-war years, when food and living conditions in the capital were particularly bad. The expulsion and extermination of the Jewish population also mainly affected Vienna where most of the Jews had lived. (The number of Viennese Jews has dwindled from 180,000 in pre-war days to some

These changes in the structure and regional distribution of industry provide new aspects in the Austrian economy which make her present-day problems rather different from those after the First World War. The addition of new industrial capacity to the Austrian economy is without doubt a positive development; so is the spreading of industrialization to areas which in the past had been neglected in this respect. But the way in which this was achieved and the way in which circumstances have changed since then have also created a number of problems which may prove difficult in the future. The main trouble lies in the fact that much of the industrial development of the past ten years was dictated by strategic and political and not by economic considerations. Thus, both the steel works in Linz and the aluminium works in Ranshofen are rather badly placed with regard to their raw material supplies, and the necessary hauls of iron-ore, coal, and bauxite are long and expensive. Also, Ranshofen has been planned for a capacity which, quite apart from the question of markets, cannot be fully utilized all year round because of the immense quantities of electricity that would be needed.[1] Again, the Zellwolle factory in Lenzing had been founded on the assumption of a continued shortage of cotton and wool. Similarly, other firms were started with little attention to the question of proper location and of production costs. Once such equipment is installed there is a tendency to protect and even expand it. This tendency has been quite noticeable in post-war Austria while some of the traditional Austrian industries which had suffered from the war economy are still lagging behind. The whole problem has not yet really come to the surface because the reconstruction demand in and outside of Austria, and the unexpected continuation of high armaments expenditures in

10,000 at the present time.) As a consequence, the population of the pre-war Vienna area (after the Anschluss a number of outlying townships were included in the Vienna area) decreased from 1,875,000 in 1934 to less than 1,500,000 in 1946, and increased gradually to over 1,530,000 in the spring of 1948. (The figures for the post-war period are based on the number of ration cards issued and are only approximately correct.)

At the same time, however, the total population of Austria has increased from 6,755,000 in 1937 to 6,953,000 at the end of 1948, largely through the influx of about half a million displaced persons. These have mainly gone to the western provinces of Austria, and have helped to swell the number of employees there,

[1] To use one-fifth of its capacity the works in Ranshofen need as much electricity as the whole federal province of Lower Austria—the biggest federal province after Vienna.

many parts of the world, have maintained a fair degree of prosperity for heavy industries all over the world. But a deterioration in this sphere would fall very heavily on Austria with her disadvantageous cost structures; and this would be particularly true if trade with the traditional Eastern European markets should not revive and Austria were to compete exclusively with the highly industrialized nations of Western Europe.

The fact that a not inconsiderable part of new industrialization in western Austria belongs to this problematic type of investment shows that the geographic redistribution also suffers from weaknesses which may create serious regional problems when the pattern of international demand undergoes changes, and competition in the field of heavy and related industries becomes more intense. These problems may well take the place of that of 'oversized Vienna' which was regarded as the principal Austrian problem after the First World War, but which by now has completely faded into the background.[1]

There is again a danger that a failure to realize these weak spots in Austria's economic structure—at present veiled by an abnormal international demand and supply situation and by the gap-filling effect of Marshall Aid—will lead to serious problems of disequilibrium later on which may cause prolonged periods of depression and difficult readjustment. It has already been mentioned that the mere existence of certain important plants has tended to secure for them protection and means of modernization and expansion which are partly lacking in those industries which had been neglected during

[1] See note 2 on p. 5. There is today—as there was after 1918—a problem of an over-sized administrative apparatus. The National Socialist period was characterized by a great bureaucratic expansion which, in spite of 'denazification', has left its mark on the second Austrian Republic. The number of persons in central and local government employment is today 367,000 compared with 298,000 in 1934. To this must be added a considerable number of persons employed by the semi-official Chambers of Industry, Agriculture, Commerce, and Labour, which also carry out public administrative functions.

An increase of 70,000 public employees over the pre-war level may not seem very great in view of the much greater amount of government intervention in economic and social matters, and it is certainly less than the relative increase in industrial employment. But it has to be remembered that the Austrian bureaucratic apparatus was already greatly oversized in pre-war days and that reform was repeatedly called for. On the whole, however, this problem of an overgrown civil service is at present by no means restricted to Austria, but is one which she has in common with many other countries, where the war and post-war period produced the same development.

the war but which will be important for a proper balance of Austria's economy in a peace-time world. Again, few attempts have been made to co-ordinate the industrial development with a foreign trade policy that will secure sufficient outlets for the industrial products and a constant inflow of the necessary food and raw material requirements.

Some of these questions may be solved with comparative ease at a later stage. Others, however, will develop in certain ways which later cannot be repaired without major and difficult socio-economic changes. Thus, the infiltration of industries into regions which have been predominantly agricultural has given a new stimulus to the rural exodus, a phenomenon that started towards the end of the last century. While post-war full employment has led to a constant increase in the number of persons employed in industry and trade, so that in 1948 employment reached a level 59 per cent higher than in 1937,[1] the number of employees in agriculture and forestry has steadily declined from a monthly average of 286,000 in 1937 to 240,000 in 1949.[2] The decline would have been far more pronounced had it not been for a considerable influx of displaced persons into agricultural jobs.[3]

NUMBER OF PEOPLE EMPLOYED IN
AGRICULTURE AND FORESTRY*

MONTHLY AVERAGES

Year	(000)
1937	285·6
1946	271·9
1947	271·0
1948	253·4
1949	240·6

* From health insurance records.

This development, particularly if it continues unchecked, will make it difficult for the Government to carry out its target of restoring food production to the pre-war level within the next three or four years and so to reduce the country's

[1] Apart from the usual seasonal fluctuations the position was practically unchanged in the first half of 1949.

[2] These figures relate only to the health-insured employees. The bulk of the man-power in the countryside is still provided by farmers and their family members. Only a small part of the latter appear on the health insurance records.

[3] In May 1947, 61,605 foreigners, of whom 41,088 were displaced persons, were employed on the land.

dependence on imports. Mechanization can of course help; and it has already helped to a considerable extent to overcome the man-power difficulties.[1] Nevertheless, the man-power shortage in agriculture is making itself seriously felt and is intensified by the fact that the rapid industrialization of the neighbouring agricultural countries has brought to an end the traditional influx of migratory workers during the summer months.

This short survey of some of the recent changes in Austria's economic life and the problems arising from them has been given in order to indicate the problems of adjustment that have to be faced by the second Republic and to avoid the misunderstanding that would arise if one thought simply of '*the* Austrian problem'; with a consequent tendency to regard the post-1945 problems as essentially the same as those after 1918, or to take 1937 as a 'normal' standard of reference for present-day developments.

WAR DAMAGES AND LOSSES

So far only those changes which were specifically Austrian have been considered. To these must be added those, like war damages and losses, which Austria has in common with other countries in Europe. Apart from war deaths, amounting to about 300,000 persons or $4\frac{1}{2}$ per cent of the pre-war population, there has also been considerable material damage to industry and housing, particularly in the industrial areas of eastern Austria which were heavily bombed and fought over. While this damage did not reach the proportions which has been characteristic of many areas in Germany, Poland, Yugoslavia, and the Soviet Union, it has probably surpassed that in most Western European countries and provides a set-back which will long be felt in production and particularly in the standards of housing and, through it, in the health and efficiency of the population.

This whole complex of Austrian and general problems has constantly to be kept in mind when turning to a more detailed picture of the major economic developments in Austria since the end of the war.

[1] See page 28.

II
1945 AND AFTER

1945: The Post-War Break-Down

WHEN the war finally ended for Austria on 8 April 1945, the economic life of the country was in complete chaos. The very complex administrative apparatus for the control of production and distribution, which the Nazis had built up and which had already shown signs of disintegration in the last months of the war, collapsed completely. In the eastern parts of the country large quantities of food, raw material stocks, and productive equipment were destroyed during the fighting or were taken to the west by the withdrawing German armies; of what was left much was requisitioned by the Red Army or plundered by the population in the first days of liberation.

Thus Vienna and the industrial areas of Lower Austria faced a complete vacuum. There were practically no food supplies at the disposal of the authorities, no administrative apparatus, or even any legal basis for obtaining such supplies from somewhere else. In these first weeks people in these areas barely survived, or not even that. Stocks of food kept in the larders at home and what could be obtained in the country-side by offering fantastic sums of money or bartering all private possessions provided that minimum by which people lived.

In May the first successful attempts were made to find a way out of the chaos. The economic legislation of the war period was taken over *en bloc*, while modifications to it and new laws were passed as the situation required. At the same time the Red Army started to support the population of Vienna by releasing foodstuffs from its own stocks. This continued until the end of August. From September onwards all four occupation Powers supplied food to Vienna (as well as to their own occupation zones), and in April 1946 Unrra began to take a decisive part in providing the necessary food-stuffs.

Even with this help, however, the level of nutrition was pitiably low. Before the war the average daily food intake of the Austrian adult amounted to 3,200 calories. During the war this was considerably reduced. In 1944 the ration of a 'normal consumer' was 2,000 calories, that of a heavy and 'heaviest' worker 2,685 and 3,403 calories respectively.[1] In May 1945 the daily ration in Vienna had fallen to 350 calories, a fraction of the minimum physiological needs. In June it could be increased to 833 calories for office workers and 1,620 calories for heavy workers. There followed some improvement in the following months, but there was a serious set-back in the spring of 1946 when internal stocks and external supplies ran out before the new harvest was brought in. From November 1946 onwards there was a slow improvement in the caloric value of the rations. But it was not until after the comparatively good harvest in 1948, and with large quantities of foodstuffs coming in under the E.R.P. programme, that rations could be raised to a level which abolished the worst hardships. In September of that year the ration of a 'normal consumer' was raised to 2,100 calories, and the average calories obtained by all rationed consumers [2] (i.e. taking account of the additional rations of workers, heavy workers, etc.) reached a level of 2,247. In June 1949 a large number of goods were taken off the ration, and the caloric value of the rations is no longer announced since they no longer indicate the whole food intake of the population. Only six groups of foodstuffs remained rationed until circumstances would permit the abolition of rationing altogether: bread and flour, meat, fats, sugar, milk and milk products, and vermicelli, rice, and semolina.[3]

[1] Unlike the British rationing system, which was fundamentally based on the idea of equal rations (with certain exceptions, such as children, expectant mothers), the German rationing system was a differential one, with different rations for children, the 'normal consumer' (mainly housewives), office workers, manual workers, heavy workers, 'heaviest' workers, and expectant mothers. Post-war Austria has taken over the German system. When in September 1948 the basic ration (of the 'normal consumer') was increased from 1,800 to 2,100 calories daily, the special group of office workers was abolished. They were included in the group of 'normal consumers'.

[2] These do not include farmers, their families, and their employees, who only got certain rationed commodities (chiefly sugar).

[3] In September 1949 some further products, such as rye-bread, cheese, and vermicelli, were derationed. By June 1950 only meat, sugar, and butter rationing remained, playing only a very modest part alongside the free market.

AUSTRIAN ECONOMY SINCE 1945

THE CALORIC VALUE OF THE AVERAGE RATION
IN VIENNA, JUNE 1945–JUNE 1949*

From		Till		Average calories per day
June	1945	August	1945 . . .	1,082
August	1945	March	1946 . . .	1,679
March	1946	May	1946 . . .	1,361
May	1946	November	1946 . . .	1,529
November	1946	August	1947 . . .	1,824
August	1947	November	1947 . . .	1,891
November	1947	June	1948 . . .	2,013
June	1948	September	1948 . . .	2,118
September	1948	June	1949 . . .	2,247

* Weighted average of the rations of all rationed consumers.

The precarious food situation in Vienna and the industrial areas of Lower Austria in the post-war period has been particularly stressed, because there the position was most serious.[1] It is true that the official rations in the western provinces were most of the time even lower than in Vienna. Nevertheless, not only were there more regular and plentiful supplies of such unrationed goods as fruit and vegetables, but rationed food, too, was more plentiful in the countryside which had escaped the ravages of war and had benefited from the wholesale transfer of cattle and stocks of food and feeding stuffs from eastern Austria.[2] Thus additional purchases in the widespread black market could be carried out at prices far below the fantastic ones charged in Vienna. Also there is a much closer personal relationship between the people in the smaller towns of western Austria and the farmers in the surrounding countryside than there is in Vienna.

[1] The same was also true for the industrial areas of Northern Styria and certain parts of Tyrol.

[2] At the end of 1945 the following changes had occurred in the three Eastern provinces (Vienna, Lower Austria, Burgenland) and in the rest of the country as compared with the end of 1944:

PERCENTAGE CHANGE IN NUMBER OF ANIMALS

	Cattle	Horses	Pigs
Eastern Austria	− 26·1	− 6·8	− 47·4
Rest of the country . . .	− 7·9	+ 23·8	− 33·5

Warning should be given at this stage that the agricultural statistics for the whole post-war period are far less reliable than pre-war statistics, since the economic controls of the Government have induced farmers to understate their acreage and production figures. (See 'Unrichtige Agrarstatistik erschwert Lenkung der Ernährungswirtschaft', in *Monatsberichte des Österreichischen Instituts für Wirtschaftsforschung*, 10/1948 (vol. 21) pp. 383-6.)

The same warning applies, though with somewhat less force, to the statistics of production and external trade.

1945 AND AFTER

The question arises, why the Government could not in these first months of extreme emergency have organized a better distribution of the available foodstuffs between west and east, and particularly between the countryside and the towns. There were several reasons. First, there was the technical difficulty arising from a completely disorganized system of transport. Between September 1944 and April 1945, 385 railway bridges had been destroyed. All the railway stations in Vienna with one exception had suffered major damage. The tramway system in Vienna, and telephone and telegraph over wide areas, had ceased to work because of technical breakdowns. Destruction and transfers to the west reduced the number of motor lorries in Vienna from 12,482 at the end of 1944 to 3,553 at the end of 1945, and that of motor cars from 17,815 to 1,786. Reconstruction work was immediately started, and before the end of 1945 pioneer troops of the Red Army and Austrian railway workers had repaired 1,600 km. of railway track, 106 bridges and tunnels, and had lifted 128 sunk ships in the Danube. Nevertheless, transport remained for many months one of the most serious bottlenecks impeding a smooth organization of production and distribution.

More serious than these technical difficulties, however, were the artificial difficulties created by the division of Austria into four occupation zones.[1] In the first post-war year each of these zones was practically a sovereign economic unit. The occupation authorities and also the Austrian provincial authorities were very reluctant to let goods pass out of their sphere of control, and extremely severe barriers hampered the intra-Austrian movement of supplies. These contrasted strangely with the lack of control at the Austrian State frontiers which made possible the export of valuable goods without the knowledge of the Austrian Government and with no or no sufficiently suitable equivalent coming into the country. This absurd state of affairs, with barter treaties, economic

[1] The four zones are: Russian zone (Lower Austria, Burgenland, and the—mainly agricultural—part of Upper Austria that lies north of the Danube); British zone (Styria and Carinthia); American zone (the industrial part of Upper Austria south of the Danube and Salzburg); French zone (Tyrol and Vorarlberg). Vienna, which came under the control of an Allied Kommandatura, was also divided into four zones, but only for occupation purposes and without any decisive administrative significance. The city of Vienna remained under the joint control of all four Allies.

boycotts, etc., disrupting the internal trade of a seven-million country, lasted for well over a year. In November 1945 a first step towards relaxation was taken when it was conceded that the laws promulgated by the Provisional Government in Vienna should be valid for the whole country. And on 28 June 1946 an Allied agreement decided on the termination of the zonal economy. But the economic administration had developed on such different lines in the various zones that it was not until the beginning of 1947 that one could talk of a unified Austrian economy.

The transport difficulties and the occupation zones were detrimental influences outside the power of the Austrian Government, but there was another, internal factor hampering a juster distribution of foodstuffs. During the war period the Nazis did not hesitate to apply the most ruthless sanctions against those who broke the regulations of economic control. Fear was thus the main mechanism on which forced deliveries, rationing, and price control had depended. Even so, there was a black market, and the last months of the war especially saw a breaking-up of the tight economic discipline. When the war was over the Provisional Government naturally hesitated to apply the same stern methods as the Nazis had used. More reliance was placed on voluntary co-operation, though legislation against economic offenders was maintained. But the long period of constant force and pressure had had a demoralizing effect on the peasants and on the business world, and relaxation of fear merely meant a greater readiness to evade the Government's orders. To this must be added the fact that the conservative Austrian People's Party, which in November 1945 emerged as the strongest party from the elections, was reluctant to enforce even those economic regulations which had been taken over or newly created by the second Republic. The black market, therefore, soon grew tremendously and, though illegal, became an established institution. In this way the Government was unable to control considerable quantities of home-produced food (or, for that matter, textiles and other industrial products) and to secure their equitable distribution.

In 1945 these factors contributed just as much to the desperate food situation in Vienna and other industrial areas as the shortage of stocks, the destruction and the requisitioning, and a harvest that was less than half the pre-war average. Had it not been for the help of the Allies and many private organizations (who did a lot for special groups of the population, particularly the children), hunger and weakness would have demanded many more victims than they actually did.

From 1948 onwards, as we saw, the food position began to improve. But the nutritional position is still far from satisfactory and is considerably worse than in pre-war days in spite of the fact that then unemployment was about four times the present level. At present [1] the average daily value of food consumed per head in Austria can be estimated at about 2,500 calories. While this already approaches normal conditions it does not reveal two important facts. First, the qualitative composition of the food consumed has considerably worsened as compared with pre-war days. Today many more of the calories are taken in the form of pulses and flour, while the consumption of proteins has considerably declined.[2] Secondly, the distribution of food consumption has become more uneven. The consumption of the peasant population has improved on its modest pre-war standards because of the war-created scarcity of useful industrial products on which they could spend what money was left after paying their debts; the very small percentage of the urban population who 'have done well' in the war and post-war period probably consume more; but the great majority of the workers and of the middle class in the towns are still living on a greatly reduced standard

[1] This refers to the autumn of 1949. Since then there has been a slight improvement.

[2] For 1947 the yearly consumption per head of the non-farm population has been estimated as follows (the figures for 1935-6 apply to the total population):

FOOD CONSUMPTION PER HEAD AND YEAR IN kg.

	1935-6	1947
Flour	116·0	131·8
Meat	57·0	15·7
Fats	14·1	10·3
Vermicelli, etc.	8·8	7·4
Pulses	2·2	6·8
Sugar	26·0	9·7
Potatoes	85·0	68·0

Since 1947 total consumption, and particularly sugar and potato consumption, have increased, but the shortage of meat and fats has continued.

since they are unable to buy any appreciable quantities of the high-priced foodstuffs.[1]

The difficulty of supplying and distributing food in the first post-war period owing to lack of transport and to the independent policy of the four occupation zones has been pointed out. It is not difficult to realize that these factors also acted as a powerful brake on the revival of industrial production, which in any case was seriously hampered (particularly in the Russian zone) by widespread destruction, requisitioning of equipment and raw materials, lack of supplies of raw materials and spare parts, and a host of other disturbing influences. The middle part of 1945 was therefore a time in which there was an unknown ebb in the output of manufactured goods. But in the midst of this apparent industrial chaos the foundations for the remarkable recovery of the coming years were laid.

The avoidance of a complete break-down of production in these first difficult post-war months was helped by two factors. The one was the large part played by artisans and small-scale enterprise in the Austrian economy. While small-scale enterprise in normal times often, but by no means always, signifies a certain backwardness in production methods and the absence of the advantages of large-scale production, it proves more adaptable, more capable of improvising in difficult times when the usual channels of supply dry up. Thus, in the first post-war months and years many small shops and artisans managed, often by ingenious methods, to keep some sort of production going and to carry out some of the immense repair work that was necessary in every field to lay the foundations of a somewhat more normal economic and social life.

The bigger enterprises, with their workshops frequently shot to pieces, with important machines missing, with irregular supplies of raw materials, with coal and electricity more often lacking than not, were in a much less favourable position to restart their complex productive mechanism on a limited scale, or to improvise with what substitute materials they could get hold of. They were put on their feet again by the tremendous efforts of the workers who, though they were

[1] The development of wages and living costs is dealt with in more detail on pp. 35-6, 47-8, 56 ff.

living on starvation rations, often with a two-hour or longer walk to and from the works, and in winter freezing at home as well as in the factories, repaired, adjusted, and rebuilt the plants instead of obtaining food and money by doing odd jobs in the country or entering the black market (as, of course, a certain minority did). This heroic effort of the first post-war year was no doubt due to the special social and political atmosphere which then prevailed. The three, then the only existing political parties (People's Party, Socialists, Communists) all co-operated, and there was a widespread will to build a new Austria. In the later post-war years, however, this promising unity weakened, and the tendency to return to pre-war economic and social conditions has endangered the spirit of reconstruction which saved Austria from complete collapse and which still is necessary to enable her to reach an early state of independence from outside help.

The great efforts of the post-war months soon began to bear fruit. Though small compared with pre-war production figures and with the immense needs of the commodity-starved post-war economy, output in many fields began to reach sizeable quantities towards the end of 1945. This was particularly true of the investment goods industries, which had been expanded during the war, but the consumer goods industries were still badly placed. An index of production covering twenty-five products of mining and basic industries calculated by the Austrian Institute for Economic Research, shows that in January 1946 production in these spheres had reached 47·8 per cent of the 1937 level. Had the consumer goods industries been included in this index, it would have been markedly lower.[1]

[1] With regard to Austrian indices of production the following remarks will be helpful. The Austrian Institute of Economic Research published the index quoted above from January 1946 to March 1948. (The dates refer to the months covered by the index, not to the dates of publication.) In June 1948 a new index was started which, beginning with January 1947, covered 47 products from both the investment and consumer goods industries. The inclusion of the consumer goods brought about a reduction in the index number as compared with the old index. Thus while the old index indicated a level of production of 70·7 (1937 = 100) for 1947, the new index only reached 61 per cent.

Another index of production, beginning with January 1948, was published by the Austrian Central Statistical Office. This is based on about seventy industrial products. This index stood permanently below the index of the Institute for Economic Research. For 1948 the index of the Institute reached 93·5 per cent of 1937, the Central Statistical Office index, however, reached only 78 per cent.

OUTPUT OF SOME COMMODITIES
JANUARY 1946 AND MONTHLY AVERAGE 1937

Commodity	Unit	Monthly average 1937	January 1946
Coal	1,000 tons	19·2	7·2
Lignite	1,000 ,,	270·1	222·3
Iron ore	1,000 ,,	157·1	5·2
Steel	1,000 ,,	54·1	4·4
Magnesite (crude) . .	1,000 ,,	33·2	0·1
Cement	1,000 ,,	35·7	9·9
Matches	1,000 boxes	11,628·0	5,122·0
Cellulose	1,000 tons	25·3	3·2
Paper	1,000 ,,	19·4	7·7

The attempt to carry on production by using all sorts of improvised methods, and the widespread mobilization of the workers for repair and reconstruction work also helped to solve the employment problem, which otherwise might have become very serious in view of the shortage of fuel and raw materials. It must also be added that many firms used their liquid financial position, which they could not turn into raw materials or equipment, to maintain their skilled personnel even during prolonged idle periods in order to be ready for production when conditions improved.

The first period after the war saw huge movements of population which not only caused considerable fluctuations in employment but also further aggravated the problem of food distribution and industrial revival. The masses of forced foreign labour which the war machine had brought to Austria

The reasons for the divergence are that the latter index includes more consumer goods, whose production lagged behind that of investment goods, and excludes —as the Institute's index does not—the production of electric energy, which in 1948 was 38 per cent above its pre-war level. There is also a difference in weighting procedure, though it is not clear whether this has a constant bias in one direction. The Central Statistical Office weighs quantities with base-year prices, where in some cases 'net prices' are substituted for actual prices, the net price being an attempt to subtract those parts of the price which are needed for raw materials. The Institute weighs individual production indices by base-year employment figures.

In what follows the old index of the Institute will be used for 1946 and the new one for the period beginning January 1947. The Institute's index is preferred because it is broken up into several sub-indices which permit a closer analysis of events. Since the *movement* of the two indices (as contrasted with their absolute level) is usually in fair agreement, and since it is mainly the movement that interests us, the conclusions derived from the one index will on the whole not be different from those derived from the other.

It should be added that beginning with November 1949 the Institute began to publish a revised index of industrial production covering a larger number of commodities and using net values of production as weights. The Central Statistical Office ceased publication of its index early in 1950.

streamed back to their home countries, while Austrian prisoners of war began to return in increasing numbers and became absorbed in the economic process. Women who had been mobilized for war work left employment, particularly because bartering in the countryside became much more important for securing the livelihood of a family than earning an additional income. Employment in Vienna [1] (for which alone figures for the whole of 1945 are available) declined rapidly from 431,100 at the end of March 1945 to 283,100 at the end of August, then rose steadily and surpassed the level of March 1945 in August 1946. But while the number of men declined from 211,900 in March 1945 to 147,800 in August and returned to its war-time level in March 1946, the number of women declined from 219,200 to 135,300 in September 1945 and 131,200 in January 1946, and never quite rose again to its war level. [2]

NUMBER OF EMPLOYED IN VIENNA IN 1945*
(000 omitted)

	Jan.	Feb.	March	Apr.	May	June
Men	219·9	216·1	211·9	210·9	197·9	165·6
Women	227·5	224·5	219·2	217·1	204·1	172·2
Total	447·3	440·6	431·1	428·1	402·0	337·8

	July	Aug.	Sept.	Oct.	Nov.	Dec.
Men	157·8	147·8	150·8	160·4	166·2	177·9
Women	157·0	135·4	135·3	138·7	141·9	141·9
Total	314·9	283·1	286·1	299·1	308·1	319·8

* Excluding caretakers and domestic servants.

When in December 1945 employment and unemployment figures for the whole country were published for the first time, it turned out that the number of employees in industry and trade in this seasonally unfavourable month was slightly greater than the monthly average of 1937 (971,900 as compared with 897,100), and that the number of registered unemployed was 80,300, i.e. considerably lower than the pre-war average (321,000 in 1937). In the following months an inflationary policy and the tremendous needs of reconstruction not only helped to swell employment by an absorption of the prisoners of war and those displaced persons who were capable and willing to work, but also quickly reduced unemployment

---

[1] Excluding caretakers and domestic servants.
[2] In November 1949 it stood at 191,800, its highest level since the war.

figures till they reached their lowest point of 39,700 in September 1947.

With all the physical destruction and disorganization, Austria inherited another difficulty from the war which proved just as great a hindrance to all reconstruction efforts: the currency chaos. During the war Germany had relied on financing her needs by constant increases in the note issue, while the inflationary effects of this policy were kept in check by a rigidly enforced price and wage stop. The inflationary pressure thus engendered, though kept in bounds, became infinitely stronger when Austria started her new economic life after the war. Not only did the goods on which the money could be spent dwindle to insignificant proportions, but also the quantity of money continued to rise. A Government budget deficit and the financial needs of an occupation army which in the first months numbered 800,000 men (reduced within a year, however, to about a quarter of this size) still further swelled the note issue. To this must be added large quantities of mark notes smuggled into Austria from neighbouring countries where they had ceased to be legal tender. It has been estimated that in the months following the end of the war some ten milliard [1] marks were circulating in Austria, compared with a note circulation of 849 million schillings in 1937. [2]

It will be clear that with such a divergence in the development of money and commodities the maintenance of a price level only moderately above that obtainable at the beginning of the war would in any case have been a difficult task. But with a Government which, as has been shown, was reluctant to use drastic measures to enforce controls, it could not work. Thus while the Government tried to take over the price and wage freeze from the war period, it soon began to permit exceptions to the principle. On the basis of 'proved' cost increases individual price rises were permitted, and though to begin with they remained within fairly modest limits, they prepared the way for steeper increases later on.

[1] Thousand million.
[2] At the Anschluss in March 1938 the schilling was exchanged at the rate of 1·5 to the mark. When in December 1945 the mark notes were replaced by schilling notes the exchange ratio was 1 : 1. This has to be remembered when present prices are compared with pre-war schilling prices. The sterling equivalent of 1 milliard schillings is for the period covered by this study £25 million at the official exchange rate.

Of far greater immediate importance, however, was the quick increase in black market operations which, though still illegal, could hardly be called clandestine. It was in this black market, which sucked away large quantities of goods from the official rationing and distribution system, that the inflation came into full play and prices soared to tremendous heights. In August 1945 an index of black-market food prices in Vienna showed them to be 264 times as high as official prices. Prices of non-essential consumer goods (cigarettes, wine, coffee, etc.) were 124 times official prices.

It was clear that something had to be done in the monetary field if more normal conditions were to be restored in trade and if the Government's control over the economy was to be more effective. But in this first chaotic post-war period, where so many questions about the political and economic future of the country seemed undecided, they hesitated—and perhaps this hesitation was justified—to enact a major immediate reform. There was also a feeling that such a reform was likely to be more successful after a certain amount of recovery in production had been achieved.

Thus only provisional measures were undertaken, which aimed at the establishment of certain minimum requirements for an ordered monetary system. In July 1945 the Austrian Central Bank, the Österreichische Nationalbank, was again put in charge of all Austrian currency and foreign exchange affairs. At the same time a law was passed (*Schaltergesetz*) which enabled the commercial banks to reopen. This law (which became effective only in the Russian zone) introduced a freezing of 60 per cent of all deposits (current and saving accounts) and limited the right of withdrawal from the remaining 40 per cent to important purposes, mainly subsistence needs of individuals or wage and raw material payments of enterprises. At the same time free withdrawal and preferred treatment at a future currency reform was promised to all deposits opened after the promulgation of the law. This led to an influx of about 1·5 milliard marks into the banks and savings banks in July and the following months.

In November 1945 a further step was taken with the passage of the Schilling Law (*Schillinggesetz*). It provided for the exchange of mark notes and Allied schilling notes against new schilling notes (with the exception of amounts below ten schillings, which were replaced later) at the rate of 1 : 1. Only 150 sch. were, however, paid out in cash while the rest was transferred to an account of which only restricted use could be made. At the same time the ideas of the earlier *Schaltergesetz* were now extended to the whole country. A rather complicated system of six different types of accounts was created according to the time at which they were deposited or to the use to which they could be put. Roughly, the effect was to block about 60 per cent of all deposits completely, while the remaining 40 per cent were partly freely available, partly only usable for cheque payments, partly they could only be withdrawn for important purposes. Money deposited after 22 December could be freely used.

When the exchange of currency took place about nine milliard marks were handed in. The rest of the marks (apart from the small denominations which remained in circulation) had been deposited after the *Schaltergesetz* in July, or were smuggled into Germany where the notes remained freely usable. Of the money handed in 150 sch. were immediately given to every individual, making in all a sum of about one milliard sch. Withdrawals from freely available accounts and releases from blocked accounts for needy individuals, wage payments, and reconstruction expenditure, soon put more money in circulation. To this accrued 1·5 milliard sch. which had to be handed over to the occupation troops at the time of the currency exchange.[1] At the end of December 1945 the currency in circulation thus amounted to 3,265 million sch.

This first reform had thus somewhat limited the amount of virulent money and had put an end to the speculative import and export of mark notes from and to neighbouring countries. But it still left a wide gap between money in circulation and the supply of goods at official prices, and left the fate

---

[1] In 1946 the occupation costs were fixed at 35 per cent (later reduced to 30, 25, and 15 per cent) of the budget expenditure (that was, at 35 per cent, approximately one milliard sch.). In the following years the reduction in the number of occupation troops and the decision of the American authorities in mid-1947 to cover their occupation costs themselves led to a considerable decrease in this item of expenditure. Though about 600 million sch. had to be voted on this score every year the amounts actually used sank to 400 in 1947 and 300 in 1948. To this must be added, however, the obligation put on Austria to look after the displaced persons which resulted in an expenditure of about 130 million sch. in 1948.

of the blocked accounts undecided. These problems were not tackled until a second reform took place two years later. There was also no emergence of a clearly thought-out national credit policy. Though a commission for the control of credit was formed when the *Schillinggesetz* was passed, it did not become an effective influence. The control remained with the banks which, though formally nationalized, continued to apply traditional standards of credit worthiness and returned to their old business connexions.

A few words remain to be said about foreign trade in these difficult post-war months. Austria is a country highly dependent on foreign trade. In 1937 Austrian imports per head of the population were higher than in any other Central European country, with the exception of Switzerland, though they were considerably lower than in most Western European and Scandinavian countries. It is obvious that with the shortages that accompanied the end of the war, imports were more urgently required than ever. But it is equally obvious that this was a period singularly unfavourable to a quick expansion of foreign trade. Not only had seven years of integration into the German war economy and the division of the world into two separate camps led to a severance of old-established commercial connexions, but also the limited production could offer very little for export, and high priority had to be given to the needs of internal reconstruction to provide a basis for bigger exports later.

In view of these difficulties it is understandable that commercial foreign trade fell practically to zero in the first months after liberation. Imports, particularly food and coal, came in through Allied (and Unrra) help, a source which still provides a decisive though a slowly declining part of the country's needs; and there was a considerable amount of 'black' exporting which was never recorded.

In August 1945 the first barter agreement was signed with Hungary, to be followed by one with Czechoslovakia, and later with Italy and Switzerland. These barter agreements were restricted to specific exchanges of limited quantities of goods, and even these were not always carried out. By the end of 1945 thirty-one such specific agreements had been concluded. In January 1946, the first month for which fuller statistics of foreign trade are available, commercial imports [1] amounted to 9·9 million sch. and the exports to 3·3 million sch.—8·1 per cent and 3·2 per cent respectively of the corresponding monthly averages in 1937, in spite of considerably increased prices at the later date. Austrian foreign trade, it is safe to say, had not got started on its post-war career when the year of liberation ended.

1946: RETURN TO A FUNCTIONING ECONOMY

The previous section has shown that while 1945 was a year of apparent economic chaos and misery it also laid the foundations for a return to a functioning economy. In 1946 Austria was far from having a smoothly functioning economic system: but that year saw the beginning of a coherent economic life with a certain recognizable regularity and method in the pattern of its sequence of events. This pattern was still one characterized by frequent jerks and break-downs. Production was hampered at every turn by the shortage of fuel and power, by insufficient and irregular supplies of raw materials of every description, and by a serious lack of skilled workers, while the remnants of zonal segregation and monetary disorder further added to the existing difficulties. Of 3,962 industrial enterprises [2] which reported on employment and production to the Chamber of Industry and Trade in August 1946, 996 were still engaged on repair work or had not started production for some other reason, while of the remaining 2,966 undertakings 59·5 per cent reported that they were operating below 50 per cent of their output capacity.

[1] The official foreign trade returns refer in principle only to the normal commercial imports and exclude imports under the various post-war relief and credit schemes. This principle is, however, not quite consistently applied. Thus the import figures always included *all* the coal imports, including relief imports, as well as all the imports under the British £10 million credit, and some of the E.R.P. imports, in particular those coming in under indirect Marshall aid from European Marshall countries. Among the items excluded foodstuffs are by far the most important. Hereinafter 'imports', without further qualification, refers to these official figures.

On the export side most exports are included except 'black' exports and part of the goods exported by the Russian-owned formerly German enterprises.

It must also be added that the valuation of the imports, and particularly of the exports, is far less reliable than in pre-war times. Under-valuation of exports and over-valuation of imports had become a widely accepted method of evading the regulations forbidding capital export. Also, in the case of barter deals, which still played a prominent part in foreign trade (about 40 per cent of all exports are barter deals), the pricing of imports and exports is of necessity often arbitrary.

[2] With at least six employees.

Nevertheless, the total picture is, in marked contrast to the first post-war period, one of a coherent rise in productive activity, despite innumerable difficulties. Apart from minor fluctuations the index of production in mining and the basic industries rose steadily from 47·8 in January 1946 to 67·3 in October (1937 = 100), i.e. by 41 per cent. In the same period employment in industry and trade rose by 35 per cent,[1] and unemployment declined steadily from 84,100 at the beginning of the year to 61,200 at the end. Since there were at the latter date 95,300 vacancies notified to the labour exchanges (a number considerably lower than the 160,000-170,000 which had been reported at the height of the labour demand season in spring and early summer), a state of full employment was approached in 1946 and finally reached in 1947, when the number of people looking for work dropped to 40,700 in the second half of the year, 2·1 per cent of the total number of employees. This was the first experience of full employment in peace-time that Austria had had since the wild inflation days after the First World War. Even so it was not complete full employment all round. Many of the vacancies were in agriculture, which did not attract the unemployed, and there were intractable pockets of unemployment in certain occupations, particularly among office staff and other white-collar workers. Their numbers had been considerably swollen under the Nazis, who had built up a considerable bureaucratic apparatus which they frequently manned even with poorly qualified Austrians, bringing in foreign labour to do the manual work.

Though the post-war period saw a relative decline in the income of this group whose wage increases lagged behind those of other workers, and whose absolute wages in many cases fell below those of manual workers exercising a comparable degree of skill, old and engrained prejudices and considerations of social prestige kept people looking for this kind of work. On a monthly average there were in 1946 28,300 white-collar workers looking for jobs, but only 2,600 suitable vacancies were notified to the labour exchanges. A broad

[1] Total employment increased by only 25 per cent, because of a falling tendency in agricultural employment, and fairly extensive reductions in the staff of the State railways and in the civil service, which continued till spring 1947 when a slight increase took place.

campaign carried out by the labour exchanges to retrain office workers for manual work, or to help them to go back to former occupations, had some success and reduced this class of unemployed to about 13,000 at the beginning of 1948.[1] But the special problem of this occupational group will remain a thorny question which will become aggravated when, with the end of occupation, the not inconsiderable number of office workers, interpreters, etc., employed by the occupation authorities [2] lose their jobs, while at the same time growing unemployment in other fields will narrow down the possibilities of retraining schemes.

But while similar special problems remained in the sphere of employment and in some fields of production, the fact remains that the general picture in 1946 was one of a tendency towards full employment and quickly expanding production. In some ways the index of production understates the progress in reconstruction achieved.

PRODUCTION AND EMPLOYMENT IN 1946

	Index of production in mining and basic industries 1937 = 100	Total employment	Employed in industry and trade (000 omitted)	Unemployed
Jan. . . .	47·8	1500·9	1011·0	84·1
Feb. . .	47·2	1539·0	1051·5	82·0
Mar.. . .	52·8	1583·3	1094·6	82·1
Apr.. . .	51·5	1631·4	1134·3	78·1
May . .	56·5	1689·8	1181·8	80·7
June . . .	57·0	1741·0	1221·7	79·9
July . . .	68·3	1791·2	1263·8	72·4
Aug.. . .	66·7	1833·8	1306·1	69·7
Sept.. . .	65·3	1840·3	1320·2	68·0
Oct.. . .	67·3	1874·7	1364·4	66·4
Nov.. . .	63·4	1879·5	1377·7	64·7
Dec.. . .	56·2	1849·5	1377·5	61·2

On the one hand it gives too optimistic a picture by leaving out agriculture and the consumer goods industries in which development lagged behind mining and the heavy industries; on the other hand it does not reflect the very considerable amount of repair and reconstruction work carried out by numerous tradesmen and artisans and by the factory

[1] Since then it has risen to about 18,000 in the first half of 1949.
[2] Their number has been estimated at 30,000, a considerable percentage of whom are displaced persons.

workers. Also, the desire to sell part of the output in the black market led to understatements in production reports.

The fact seems to be (though it would be difficult to substantiate this statement by accurate figures) that 1946, and even more 1947 and 1948, were years with a total production below, and living standards far below, pre-war levels, while at the same time capital formation exceeded that of pre-war years. This fact would not only explain the relatively quick increase in production in a badly war-shattered economy; it also helps to explain, and is in turn underlined by the very uneven *post-war* development of investment goods and consumer goods industries, the first of which exceeded the 1937 production as early as March 1948 (by 11 per cent) while the latter had by that date only reached 59·6 per cent of the pre-war level.

A high degree of capital formation, even at the cost of reducing consumption to very low levels,[1] can of course easily be justified as an emergency policy for a country which has to rebuild its economic foundations and which has to try to emancipate itself from very extensive external help. But much of the capital formation carried out in Austria in these first years of recovery was haphazard, and much of it was wasted from the viewpoint of the national economy, though it may have been profitable for the individual investor.[2] Scarce building materials and building labour were used for building more beautiful barns for prosperous peasants, and showy shop fronts and night clubs, while hundreds of factories were still working under leaking roofs and without glass windows. Even where investment took the form of productive expansion it was by no means always the more urgent projects which obtained priority. Considerable numbers of new firms were started to exploit short-lived boom conditions for certain substitute commodities, investments which were bound to prove useless as soon as more normal conditions returned.[3] In general there was also a tendency to invest 'in width' rather than 'in depth', i.e. to create new plant (which was not

[1] This development was greatly helped by an inflationary monetary policy to which we shall return later.

[2] By enabling him to escape the loss of his savings through inflation, or to make huge profits during the short-lived post-war boom.

[3] As a curiosity it may be mentioned that more than 200 film companies were entered in the trade register in the first post-war period many of which, of course, never started production, while others soon ran into heavy losses.

fully utilized because of the shortage of raw materials) instead of modernizing and expanding existing plant, which in many cases would have been more useful.

We can, nevertheless, say that 1946, and the same goes for 1947, saw a very marked recovery in industrial production and in the volume of capital formation. In two other fields vital for Austria's economy, however, in agriculture and foreign trade, recovery lagged seriously behind industrial production, and the retardation there was mainly responsible for the continued economic plight of Austria in these years.

The total lack of stocks and the reduced import opportunities made an increased harvest in 1946 a matter of vital interest to Austria. That it would not be possible to return straight away to pre-war results was obvious. Less acreage was under cultivation and throughout the war years the soil had been exploited without sufficient fertilizing. In 1946 the

USE OF ARTIFICIAL FERTILIZERS
CONSUMPTION OF PURE NUTRITIVE SUBSTANCE
(000 tons)

	Nitrogen	Phosphoric acid	Potash
1937	6·7	14·0	8·6
1946	7·6	2·8	6·6
1947	9·5	13·1	7·0
1948	21·8	18·8	12·3

supply of artificial fertilizers had become even more inadequate, while at the same time the reduction in the number of cattle meant a loss of manure. The shortage of labour added to the difficulties, particularly in the case of sugar beet production, but it was partly overcome by the delivery through Unrra of 727 light and 140 heavy tractors [1] together with many other

[1] As the incorporation of Austria into Germany had also led to a considerable increase in the sales of agricultural machinery, post-war Austrian agriculture is far more mechanized than pre-war as the following figures show:

AGRICULTURAL MACHINERY

	1939	1946
	(no. of units)	
Electrical motors	88,051	142,526
Combustion motors	38,892	44,237
Tractors	1,782	7,465
Sowing machines	40,724	53,892
Binders	1,955	8,564
Other harvesters	39,547	49,659
Potato harvesters	6,193	35,564

types of agricultural machinery,[1] and also by attracting many temporary workers from the towns by large food bonuses.

To all these difficulties, which were a consequence of the war and thus did not come unexpectedly, were added catastrophic droughts in 1946 and 1947, which postponed agricultural recovery till 1948, so that 1949 was the first year with more normal conditions. The consequence was that while all economic indices were rising, agricultural production declined to disastrously low levels. Even though the official figures overstate the decline, since they are based on returns which deliberately try to hide the extent of agricultural production,[2] they nevertheless give a picture of events which, though exaggerated, is essentially correct. It shows that yields per hectare [3] had declined in the case of wheat to 71 per cent (1946) and 58 per cent (1947) of the 1937 level, in the case of rye to 80 per cent and 74 per cent, in the case of potatoes to 59 per cent and 47 per cent. Similar declines were reported for the other agricultural products. Since, in addition, land that used to be under the plough had been turned over to grassland,[4] the quantities of basic foodstuffs harvested declined even more catastrophically. Bread grains (wheat and rye) declined in 1946 and 1947 to 53·8 and 44 per cent of the 1937 quantities, coarse grains (maize, barley, oats) to 39·8 and 33·8 per cent, potatoes to 42·4 and 30·3 per cent, and sugar beet to 22·3 and 25·3 per cent.[5]

Some of the tractors and agricultural machinery delivered by Unrra could not be used later on because the necessary spare parts were not available. On the other hand a considerable domestic industry for agricultural machinery has sprung up since the end of the war; a large part of the products of which are available for the home market. Thus the Steyr works were producing 401 tractors a month in the January-May period of 1949 compared with only nine tractors a month on the 1937 average and thirty-four in 1947. The tonnage of other agricultural machinery produced was on the average of the first four months of 1949, 42 per cent above the 1937 monthly average.

[1] Most of the fertilizers were also obtained through the help of Unrra.

[2] This explains the strange fact that if all the reports about the usage (or non-usage) of the land are added together a considerable part of Austria's cultivable area seems to have vanished, and also explains the over-delivery of agricultural products as compared with the delivery quotas based on the official statistics.

[3] 1 hectare = 2·74 acres.

[4] Which requires less labour, offered a substitute for the lack of imported feeding stuffs, and was more profitable since animal products could be more easily sold in the black market and secured high prices there.

[5] It may be mentioned here that before the war Austria could cover about 75 per cent of her food requirements out of her own production.

AGRICULTURAL PRODUCTION IN 1937, 1946, AND 1947

	Area cultivated	Yield per hectare	Total yield
1937	(000 hectares)	(tons)	(000 tons)
Wheat . .	250	1·60	400·3
Rye . .	358	1·33	476·7
Barley . .	167	1·72	288·1
Oats . .	287	1·65	474·8
Maize . .	70	2·95	206·3
Potatoes .	216	16·76	3,611·7
Sugar-beet .	40	24·96	1,007·6
1946			
Wheat . .	200	1·14	227·5
Rye . .	229	1·07	244·4
Barley . .	115	0·98	112·4
Oats . .	199	0·95	188·1
Maize . .	52	1·64	85·3
Potatoes .	156	9·82	1,532·8
Sugar-beet .	16	13·98	225·0
1947			
Wheat . .	183	0·93	169·5
Rye . .	221	0·98	216·2
Barley . .	103	0·92	94·3
Oats . .	191	0·90	173·1
Maize . .	50	1·22	60·5
Potatoes .	139	7·88	1,095·0
Sugar-beet .	21	11·94	254·8

This reduction in the amount of home-grown food meant that in spite of the very low rations the bulk of the food for the non-farm population had to be imported. In 1946, 39 per cent of the calories distributed in the form of rations to this section of the population came from domestic sources, 1 per cent from commercial imports and 60 per cent from Unrra and the occupation forces. In 1947 the proportion covered by Unrra and American relief credits was even greater.

Thus, while the large-scale relief measures from abroad helped to avoid the nutritional crisis which would have followed the decline in agricultural production, this decline had the bad effect of forcing Austria to use most of the relief grants offered to her for immediate subsistence needs, leaving too little for the important raw material and capital equipment requirements of industry. Thus, of the $90 million Unrra goods delivered in 1946, about 78 per cent consisted of food-stuffs and another 12 per cent of supplies for agriculture, leaving only insignificant sums for industrial reconstruction. And even two years later in the first Marshall Aid year (April 1948—March 1949), more than half of the $280 million aid had to be used for essential food and agricultural supplies. The long drawn-out agricultural crisis and the failure to control more effectively the existing domestic supplies thus resulted not only in a low standard of living for a large part of the population, but also in a loss of opportunities for the long-term reconstruction of Austria's economy.

Though foreign trade was listed as the other important sphere of Austria's economic life the development of which lagged behind industrial recovery, it presents a very different picture from agriculture. In contrast to the actual decline of the latter, foreign trade showed a very strong upward trend from the first months of 1946 which has lasted, though with a diminishing rate of growth, till the present day. From January 1946 till July 1946 imports increased from 9·9 million sch. to 30·1 million sch. and exports from 3·3 million sch. to 30·6 million sch. After this there followed a stationary period (apart from heavy seasonal and irregular fluctuations) until in the spring of 1947 a new upward movement got under way.

But impressive as the more than ninefold increase of export values in the first seven months of 1946 must appear, it was still only a small and very insufficient beginning in relation to the external trading needs of Austria. Two things have to be remembered when looking at these figures. First, a not inconsiderable part of the rise merely reflects the rise in prices that took place in this period,[1] and secondly, commercial trade had practically fallen to zero point in 1945 so that a very steep advance was necessary if the same relative position (i.e. relative to pre-war days) as that of the other indices of economic life was to be reached. Thus, when in the last quarter of 1946 a more detailed break-down of foreign trade figures permitted for the first time the calculation of a volume index of foreign trade,[2] it turned out that (commercial) imports had only reached 11 per cent and exports 13 per cent of the 1937 volume.[3]

[1] See p. 36, below. Another factor which played a certain part in making the statistical progress appear bigger than the real progress was the improvement in the collection of foreign trading figures by the customs authorities.

[2] i.e. a valuation of imports and exports at stable (in this case 1937) prices.

[3] The volume index used here is the quarterly index published by the Austrian Institute of Economic Research. A monthly volume index is calculated by the Austrian Central Statistical Office which does not, however, give regularly a break-down into major commodity groups, as the former index does. The two indices correspond closely with each other, minor deviations originating from slight differences in the method of calculation.

VALUE OF IMPORTS AND EXPORTS IN 1946
(million sch.)

	Imports	Exports
Jan.	9·9	3·3
Feb.	11·9	3·4
March	10·1	3·6
April	16·7	9·4
May	18·5	22·0
June	18·0	17·2
July	30·1	30·6
August	34·0	13·9
Sept.	30·3	27·8
Oct.	19·3	27·0
Nov.	24·2	30·9
Dec.	27·9	30·2

But while these figures reveal clearly the long way foreign trade had still to go—a truth also shown by the fact that of the goods originating from abroad and available to Austria in 1946 only about 11 per cent were normal commercial imports, the remaining 89 per cent coming from Unrra, the occupation authorities, American war surplus credits, and charitable organizations—it is still possible to say that in foreign trade as well, 1946 represents a return to a functioning economy. For small though the volume of trading was, the foundations were laid for a more normal basis of foreign trading. The individual barter deals which had characterized foreign trade in 1945 now gave way to some extent to more flexible bilateral clearing agreements and to sales and purchases against freely convertible currencies. Trading and/or payments agreements were concluded with Switzerland, Italy, Great Britain, France, Belgium, the Netherlands, and Poland. The immediate effects of these agreements were small, mainly because of the very limited exportable surpluses of Austria's industries. In the beginning trade was mainly developed with Switzerland who took 36 per cent of Austria's exports (compared with 5·1 per cent in 1937)and provided 31 per cent of the imports (3·2 per cent in 1937); apart from coal imports from Germany, two other neighbouring countries, Italy and Czechoslovakia accounted for the bulk of the remaining trade. But the importance of the trade treaties lay in the fact that they paved the way for the resumption of old trade connexions and permitted the accumulation of experience for the conclusion of further treaties suited to the changed circumstances. After a comparatively quiet period in 1947 numerous negotiations were started in 1948, and by the middle of 1949 trade treaties had been established with sixteen, mainly European countries, as compared with thirty-two countries in 1937. The restitution of the overseas treaties had still to be accomplished.

This whole return to a more integrated economic life, which can be considered as a characteristic aspect of the 1946 developments, took place against a background of loosening anti-inflationary checks. The *Schillinggesetz* of December 1945 had laid the foundations for an autonomous monetary policy and had also reduced the active note circulation, though not sufficiently to adjust it to the reduced production valued at official prices. But even this oversized currency volume was soon expanded. Sums on the blocked accounts were successively released in order to supplement the insufficient incomes of old-age pensioners and other needy persons, and particularly for wage and reconstruction expenditure of expanding firms. From the end of October till the end of December 1946, when the figures for the blocked accounts at the Austrian National Bank (belonging mainly to the other banks and public bodies) were first published, they decreased from 4,210 million sch. to 4,015 million sch. Then, on the free accounts, too, there was a considerable amount of dissaving. Fear of a currency reform and the need to supplement the short rations by purchases in the black market led to considerable withdrawals of money. At the Viennese banks and saving institutions 1·2 milliard sch. were withdrawn (from free and blocked accounts) in the course of 1946. Finally, Government expenditure further added to the growing volume of means of payment. Though the ordinary budget for 1946 was balanced, there was an extraordinary budget for reconstruction expenditure [1] which was to be financed by deficit spending. In actual fact the revenue turned out to be higher and the ordinary expenditure lower than expected so that the deficit on the extraordinary budget came only to 76 million sch. instead of an expected 274 million sch. But these 76 million sch. do not cover the expenditure for the occupation forces and the displaced persons. This was raised by Treasury Bills which were taken up not so much by individuals or industry, but predominantly by financial institutions. This, however, had an inflationary

[1] This also applies to the following years.

effect, partly by bringing into circulation idle money hoards, partly by forcing the banks, whose liquidity was reduced by the growing withdrawals, to turn to the National Bank for a release of their blocked accounts or for a re-discount of their Treasury Bills.

BUDGET FOR 1946
(million sch.)

EXPENDITURE	Estimated	Actual
Ordinary	2,526·0	2,465·9
Extraordinary	278·2*	303·4*
REVENUE	2,530·2	2,693·6
Surplus on ordinary account . .	4·2	227·7
Total deficit	274·0	75·7

* Excluding expenditure for the occupation forces and the displaced persons.

All these influences taken together made for a constant upward pressure on the note circulation which did not meet any determined resistance from the Government or the Austrian National Bank. Thus from January till the end of the year the note circulation increased by 61 per cent, from 3,463 million sch. to 5,561 million sch.

NOTE CIRCULATION IN 1946
(million sch.)

Jan. . . 3,463	May . . 4,732	Sept. . . 5,101
Feb. . . 4,007	June . . 4,889	Oct. . . 5,149
March . . 4,206	July . . 5,090	Nov. . . 5,282
April . . 4,287	Aug. . . 5,187	Dec. . . 5,561

It is clear that such an increase in the volume of the currency could not but make itself felt in the price level. While many individual price increases had been granted in 1945, 1946 saw large-scale price and wage movements, typical of strong inflationary pressure. An additional factor making for rising prices was the arbitrary fixation of the schilling rate at 10 : 1 to the dollar and 40 : 1 to the pound. The advantage of a round figure in making calculations easy, as well as the normal desire of an occupying force to overvalue its own currency, combined to result in this exchange rate which greatly undervalued the schilling.[1] The consequence was that

[1] In 1937 the schilling-dollar rate had been 5·34 : 1. Official prices had risen rather less in Austria between 1937 and 1945 than in most countries.

On the black market, the dollar, the pound, the Swiss franc, and a number of other currencies were sold at about seven to eight times the official rate, but this was largely due (1) to the desire to flee from the unstable schilling to more stable currencies, and (2) to the fact that certain goods were not available at all in Austria or only at fantastic black market prices.

prices of imported goods were generally above the internal price level. (But these goods could still be easily sold because of the small supply of goods at official prices). Exports, of course, were stimulated by this exchange rate,[1] but this stimulation did not carry any economic advantages for the country as a whole, because in this period production bottle-necks provided a far more important check to exports than high prices. In fact, this exchange rate contributed in the early period of reconstruction to very unfavourable barter terms of trade for the Austrian economy.

Attempts were made to reduce the rise in prices caused by the low schilling valuation. An important measure was the sale of the foodstuffs imported under the various relief schemes not at their world market prices but at the lower (and subsidized) internal prices. This covered the larger part of imports. For the rest a compensation pool was created into which exporters should pay the excess profits which resulted from the higher prices they could gain abroad, these payments then to be used for subsidizing imports. This scheme, however, met with strong opposition from the export trade, and had only a short and precarious life without ever achieving its aim. Later the rise in prices brought the Austrian price level more into line with world prices and in 1948 the problem began to turn from that of an under-valued schilling to that of an over-valued schilling as more and more exporters found difficulties in disposing of their goods in foreign markets. The official exchange rate was, however, continued though an actual devaluation of the schilling was achieved firstly, by continuing barter trade, which leads to specific exchange rates depending on the relative prices of the bartered goods in the two bartering countries, and secondly, by the growth of a system of premiums paid by importers to exporters for foreign exchange, which gained the approval of the National Bank which took part in its administration. On 22 November 1949 the schilling was officially devalued and a system of multiple exchange rates introduced.

To return to 1946, it has been seen that at that period the

---

[1] This is true as far as official prices are concerned. In the domestic black market, prices were often more profitable than in the export market. In view of the insufficient control over the distribution of materials and their use, this proved to be one of the hindrances to a quicker expansion of exports.

schilling was still under-valued and this added to the upward movement of prices. The cost-of-living index,[1] which between April 1945 and June 1946 had only increased by 14 per cent, jumped in the second half of that year by another 26 per cent.[2] Wages also began to break through the wage stop in an attempt to catch up with the rising prices. In two big waves, one in the spring of 1946 and one towards the end of the year, wage claims were pressed forward, and in December 1946 the index of net wages in Vienna[3] was 59 per cent above the level of April 1945.

Thus, just as production began to recover, the official wage-price structure began to show signs of growing disequilibrium.

PRICES AND WAGES IN VIENNA IN 1946

	Cost-of-living index	Net wage-rates	Food prices on the black market
	April 1945 = 100		August 1945 = 100
April . .	113	115	76
May . .	113	118	69
June . .	114	120	66
July . .	122	129	50
August .	123	131	39
September .	126	131	29
October .	135	138	26
November .	142	140	24
December .	144	159	27

WINTER 1946-7: THE GREAT SET-BACK

The tender blossoms of recovery that had begun to show in 1946 were almost destroyed in the winter of that year before they could substantially develop.

[1] This index is based on the pre-war expenditure of a working-class family with two children. For the period reviewed by this paper it is an unsatisfactory guide to the study of price movements and living costs, because it contains a high proportion of heavily subsidized goods whose prices had risen less than other goods, and because rationing meant that only a limited amount of goods could be obtained at the recorded prices.

[2] Only black market prices came down from the absurd heights they had reached in 1945. Shortage of money following the *Schillinggesetz* as well as increased supplies coming into the towns from the countryside reduced black market prices in Vienna from 264 times the official prices in August 1945 to 43 times that level in December 1946.

[3] This is a weighted index of wage-rates of skilled and unskilled male and female workers after deduction of tax and social insurance contributions calculated for an earner with three dependants (wife and two children).

The severe drought of the summer which, as has been seen, had dashed all hopes of an early recovery in agriculture, also had a bad effect on electricity production. The hydro-electric works, which supply about 86 per cent of Austria's electricity, found their supplies of water dwindling and already in autumn—much earlier than usual—production went down heavily. On top of this came an early and hard winter which froze the water supplies from the glaciers earlier than usual. In February 1947 electricity supplied from the hydro-electric works had fallen to 34 per cent of the level reached in the previous July. Frantic efforts to fill the gap by coal-generated electricity had only modest results, partly because of insufficient and irregular coal supplies, partly because of the limited capacity of the badly damaged caloric electricity works. Total electricity production thus declined in the same period to 53 per cent of the July level.

This break-down in electricity supplies was transformed into a general fuel crisis of unknown dimensions by a simultaneous decline in coal imports. These, which had in July 1946 only reached 78 per cent (214,307 tons) [1] of the monthly average of imports in 1937, declined rapidly until in February 1947 they had fallen to 131,845 tons or 48 per cent of the monthly average in 1937. Domestic production could be maintained at a more stable level, but since it only played a very secondary part in meeting the country's coal requirements, it could not prevent a decline of 25 per cent in the total amount of coal available (domestic production plus imports) between July and February from 323,413 tons to 243,762 tons.

If one adds to this decline in fuel and power supplies (which had been scarce before) the fact that the energy requirements of industry and households are increased in winter, the repercussions of this break-down can be imagined. While the population was shivering in unheated rooms and places of work, fuel supplies for production had also to be severely curtailed. Already in September enterprises were advised to

---

[1] Since brown coal (lignite) provides the major part of Austria's domestic fuel and is also extensively imported, all the figures relating to coal imports and production include brown coal, coal, and coke. The quantities are added up on a coal basis', i.e. 2 tons of brown coal = 1 ton of coke = 1 ton of coal. This allows in a rough and ready manner for the poorer quality of brown coal.

cut down their consumption of electric energy to 80 per cent of the June level. The following month saw further restrictions and in January an emergency programme had to be worked out to secure the minimum requirements of fuel and power for the most essential industries at the expense of the others. Even this emergency programme, however, could not be fully maintained during the two most crucial months, January and February 1947. The index of production fell from 68 in July 1946 to 45 in February 1947. Even this gives a very incomplete picture of the effects of the fuel crisis as this index contains predominantly mining and those basic industries whose production was maintained at the expense of the other industries. The decline in the production of the less essential industries, for which production figures are not available, was far more severe, at first because of the lack of fuel and later also because of increased bottlenecks in the supply of raw materials and intermediate products.

Transport, which had made good progress in the repair of railway track and rolling stock, was also severely hit by the shortage of coal. A decision was rightly taken to maintain as far as possible the goods traffic so as not to disturb still further the tottering structure of production. This meant, however, a concentration of economy measures on passenger traffic, which was drastically reduced causing still more congestion in the few trains running than had existed before. The ton-kilometres of passenger traffic transported by the Federal Railways fell from 58·6 million in September 1946 [1] to 16·9 million in February 1947, i.e. by 71 per cent.

This crisis in production and transport had practically no effect on a field in which big repercussions might have been expected: on employment. The number of employees in industry and trade declined only from 1,377,700 in November 1946 (the highest level reached in that year) to 1,350,500 in February 1947, a decline well within the limits of the normal seasonal recession. The reason for this abnormal divergence between production and employment figures was that employers, in possession of considerable liquid funds and aware of the general labour shortage, tried to maintain

[1] The figure was still higher for August. This month is not, however, a useful basis for comparison because its passenger traffic is swollen due to holiday travel

their labour force intact for the after-crisis resumption of production.

The shock of the fuel crisis of that winter constituted a lesson that was quickly learnt. To secure an adequate supply of fuel became one of the top priority questions of economic policy. Negotiations with the Allies for regular and reliable

THE WINTER CRISIS OF 1946-7

Electricity generated (mill. kwh.)	Coal resources* (Production and imports) (000 tons)	Index of mining and basic industrial production 1937 = 100	PRODUCTION				FEDERAL RAILWAYS		Employment in industry and trade (000 persons)
			Paper (000 tons)	Cement (000 tons)	Bricks (mill. units)	Beer (000) hectol†	Ton km. transported (millions)		
							Passengers	Freight	
327·7	323·4	68	9·43	40·6	19·3	218·4	54·1	281·0	1,263·8
290·0	315·0	67	8·74	38·7	25·5	191·9	60·3	322·1	1,306·1
269·5	276·9	65	8·24	39·5	25·5	133·5	58·6	288·4	1,320·2
231·6	260·2	67	8·57	39·0	27·0	95·3	44·4	295·5	1,364·4
220·6	296·3	63	8·10	32·3	18·7	87·4	26·6	290·8	1,377·7
225·7	302·8	56	5·78	25·2	7·8	87·8	26·6	260·1	1,377·5
192·8	267·3	46	5·13	12·0	1·6	62·3	19·2	207·8	1,358·7
174·2	243·8	45	4·17	8·2	0·6	41·4	16·9	207·9	1,350·5
223·7	306·4	62	7·27	16·3	0·4	97·6	22·0	335·6	1,362·7
261·1	247·8	70	10·17	28·1	2·1	122·8	25·0	359·0	1,381·2
303·7	339·0	74	10·10	30·9	6·3	186·5	36·5	388·7	1,397·0
303·6	349·6	77	10·59	32·4	12·6	186·4	38·3	381·1	1,401·5

* Calculated on a coal basis. See note on p. 37.
† 1 hectol = 100 l. = 22 gallons.

supplies of Ruhr coal,[1] and extended agreements for the purchase of Polish coal and Czech and Hungarian lignite, together with a stepping up of home production, soon resulted in a remarkable improvement in fuel supplies. Coal imports surpassed the monthly average of 1937 for the first time in August 1947 and have since then risen to more than 50 per cent above that level. Domestic production reached the 1937 mark in November 1948 and has since remained at a level slightly above it. As a consequence total coal supplies which

[1] Which was partly compensated by sending electric current from Austria to Germany, partly by a British £2 mill. grant and American relief credits, and which later became the most important item in Austria's indirect Marshall Aid purchases.

had only stood at 66 per cent of 1937 in 1946, rose to 86 per cent in 1947, 132 per cent in 1948, and 161 per cent in the first half of 1949.[1]

The view could even be submitted that perhaps too much attention was given to coal imports which have crowded out many other important raw material imports and have used up a very large part of interim and E.R.P. aid.[2] However, whether this view is correct or not, the immediate aim of avoiding another collapse was achieved. When in 1947 another drought cut down supplies from the hydro-electric works it looked as if a new fuel crisis of similar dimensions as in 1946 would break out. But the increasing supplies of coal coming in in the autumn of that year helped to stave off the beginnings of the threatening crisis, while a mild and wet winter provided hydro-electricity at a seasonally unexpected time. Minor curtailments of power allocation were necessary but a second reverse was avoided.

1947: INFLATION

The set-back of the fuel crisis was overcome much sooner than was expected at the time. With the recovery of electricity production in spring 1947 and increasing coal supplies, the progress in production was quickly taken up where it had been left in the summer of 1946. This applied particularly to the heavy industries and mining which had been kept going, as far as possible, even during the worst winter months. The index of production covering these industries, with 70 per cent of the 1937 production in April 1947 surpassed the highest level reached in 1946 (68 in July) and rose to a new

[1] Even with this great improvement in 1949, coal supplies were still only 84 per cent of those in 1929. Since 1929 was much nearer a full-employment economy than 1937 it may seem a better standard for judging present-day fuel requirements. This is, however, not true because considerable changes have occurred since then. Firstly, there was a great deal of wasteful coal usage in 1929 that was eradicated in the rationalization drive of the depression years. More important is the great change-over to electricity and oil as sources of power that has taken place in the past twenty years.

While thus the coal consumption of 1937 certainly under-states the needs of a fully employed Austrian economy, the 1929 figure over-states them. The truth is that by 1949 the unlimited demand for coal disappeared ; instead growing attention was given to quality and price. This created a serious problem for some of the newly expanded Austrian brown-coal mines.

[2] In 1947 14 per cent of aggregate imports (commercial and relief imports) were accounted for by coal compared with 7 per cent in 1937.

height of 84 in July. For the rest of the year, owing to seasonal declines and shortages in electricity supplies, it remained at an average of 76. In some fields progress was more spectacular than this, particularly in pig-iron production which surpassed the 1937 monthly average in every month from July 1947 onwards, after having reached only 15 per cent of the 1937 rate in 1946 and 31 per cent in the first half of 1947.

The recovery in the basic industries was, however, not paralleled by a similar recovery in the consumer goods industries. A new index of production calculated for the first time for 1947 and including a number of consumer goods industries shows that in that year the investment goods industries (which include most items of the old index plus some additional ones) reached an output of 84 per cent of 1937, but the consumer goods industries only one of 42 per cent. The combined index gives an output of 61 per cent of 1937 for the whole year and of 69 per cent for December 1947.

This increase in production to just over two-thirds of the 1937 output in the second half of 1947 was, however, only accomplished by throwing into production a very large quantity of basic resources. Employment in industry and trade increased rapidly from 1,358,700 in January to 1,422,200 in November, a figure 59 per cent above the 1937 monthly average; coal supplies in the second half of 1947 were 6 per cent higher than the 1937 average, and the ton-kilometres of freight transported by the Federal Railways in the same period 18 per cent higher than in 1937. This discrepancy between an input of labour, fuel, and transport services well above 1937 and an output well below the pre-war level shows the great shortcomings under which production had still to operate. Insufficient raw material supplies and lack of stocks causing frequent hold-ups and constant below-capacity working, cross-transport to barter scarce commodities, an undue amount of repair and maintenance work to keep intact war-damaged or improvised machinery, all contributed to an overall decline in economic productivity which was further aggravated by such factors as out-of-date machinery, and a decline in skills and labour productivity owing to bad housing and living conditions and the after-effects of war-strain and neglected education. Inflation also contributed to a neglect of cost considerations.

This decline in productivity was not an important danger to begin with. Perhaps what had to be achieved first was a quick recovery in production, no matter at what cost. But with the further progress and consolidation in production in the following years and the pressing needs for higher living standards at home and greater competitive strength in a world that turned from a sellers' market into a buyers' market, the question of productivity has become a very urgent one for Austria's economy. There has been some progress, but there is still a considerable gap between the present and pre-war days. If one takes the ratio between the index of production and an index of employment covering approximately the same industries as a very rough guide for the development of post-war productivity, it appears to have reached 51 per cent of the 1937 level in 1947, 69 per cent in 1948 and 75 per cent in the first five months of 1949.[1]

External trade, too, resumed its upward trend in spring 1947. The values of imports and exports both rose sharply and in September (imports) and October (exports) surpassed the monthly average value of 1937. And in December, the best month of the year, exports were more than five times the January value. But much of this rise was due to the inflationary rise in prices. The volume of exports rose only by 57 per cent between the first and last quarter, and had reached, in the latter period, only 40 per cent of the 1937 volume.

In foreign trade, as elsewhere, lack of co-ordination sometimes resulted in uneconomic methods. Thus, for instance, heavy industry exported its raw or semi-manufactured products in order to obtain fuel and raw materials,[2] while the engineering industries, which could have earned considerably more foreign exchange by turning those products into finished commodities, had to refuse foreign orders for lack of supplies. Again, textile firms, chocolate factories and other consumer goods industries, unable to obtain sufficient foreign exchange for their raw materials, found it necessary to work up raw

---

[1] In the first quarter of 1950 this index had climbed to 85 per cent.

[2] To encourage exports a system had been evolved which allows exporters to use part of their foreign exchange proceeds (the other part must be sold to the National Bank) for their own purchases abroad without having to go through the usual complicated procedure for the acquisition of foreign exchange for raw material requirements.

materials for foreign, mainly Swiss firms, a procedure [1] that usually involves the acceptance of less favourable terms than the ordinary export business and prevents the producing firm from establishing its own trade connexions with the middlemen and the consumers. Finally, the numerous barter deals [2] carried out side by side with clearing and foreign exchange transactions and a certain flight of capital to hard currency areas further worsened the effectiveness of the export trade.

An export volume of only 27 per cent of 1937 (for the whole of 1947) and a particularly bad harvest meant, of course, that a large part of even the most essential imports could not be paid for out of current export proceeds. The deficit had to be even greater in view of the fact that inessential imports were also admitted (partly unavoidably as concessions in trade treaties, partly due to the ineffectiveness of control, partly as a premium to exporters, who bartered them and sold them at high prices on the domestic market [3]); and also because the traditional 'invisible' incomes of Austria's balance of payments —from transit trade and tourist traffic—had recovered even less than exports. Tourist traffic, which in 1937 brought in almost 200 million sch. (1937-) resulted in 1947 in a net income of foreign exchange of not much more than 2 million sch. (1947-). Even in summer 1948, when greater efforts were made to bring in tourists, which had some success in Britain and the Netherlands, the number of foreign tourists (60,000 to 70,000 with about 450,000 days' stay) only reached a tenth of the pre-war level. Certain simplifications in payments procedure which have been introduced since then, an agreement concluded with Western Germany in August 1949 to enable German tourists to travel in Austria, and the greater availability of hotel accommodation that will follow the end of occupation, will all help to achieve quick progress in this field. But it will be a long task to restore to the tourist trade something of its pre-war significance.

Low exports and an insignificant transit and tourist trade

[1] The German term for this transaction is *Lohnveredlungsgeschäft*. The payment is usually in the form of raw materials. In 1947 about 9 per cent of all exports belonged to this group.

[2] Accounting for about 40 per cent of all exports in 1947, and probably for a similar proportion (out of an increased export volume) in 1948 and 1949.

[3] Although put in the past tense these and some other statements in this section also apply to the present period.

therefore meant a big gap in the balance of payments. It probably amounted in 1947 to more than two milliard sch., or almost 2½ times the value of exports. This gap was covered by Unrra deliveries (447 million sch.), various American grants and credits (1,050 million sch.), British credits (379 million sch.), and the contributions of charitable organizations (130 million sch.).

PRODUCTION AND FOREIGN TRADE

1947

	Total production index	Investment goods industries	Consumer goods industries	Commercial Imports	Exports	Volume of Imports	Exports
	(1937 = 100)			(million sch.)		(1937 = 100)	
Jan.	37	53	24	41·0	23·6		
Feb.	39	52	28	43·1	27·9	15	16
Mar.	52	72	36	74·1	45·5		
April	60	83	41	89·4	46·0		
May	64	89	44	95·7	64·2	25	26
June	69	93	49	100·6	74·7		
July	70	99	47	114·3	71·7		
Aug.	69	100	43	111·1	68·6	28	27
Sept.	65	89	45	121·5	75·5		
Oct.	69	92	50	131·7	102·9		
Nov.	69	91	51	125·0	116·7	32	40
Dec.	69	95	48	143·8	125·2		

BALANCE OF PAYMENTS 1947

(in million sch.)

Payments		Receipts	
Imports *	3,054	Exports	842
Services	33	Export of electricity	64
Financial transactions	14	Services †	142
Tourist trade	10	Financial transactions †	50
		Tourist trade	5
		Deficit covered by foreign grants and credits	2,008
	3,111		3,111

* Including all relief imports.
† These two items were partly swollen by payments of the American occupation authorities and transfers of past earnings of Austrian prisoners of war in the United States.

As the year 1947 proceeded it became clear that the progress made in production and foreign trade was in danger of being interrupted or distorted through the growing inflationary tendencies. The inflationary trend of 1945 and 1946, though carrying with it the usual drawbacks of an unjust distribution of incomes and monetary burdens, and of uneconomic investments, had acted as a stimulant to reconstruction. But in 1947 this inflationary trend gathered momentum and memories of the run-away inflation of 1920-2 began to haunt wide circles of the population. Transfer of capital, hoarding of goods, investments at any cost, and other attempts at a 'flight from the Schilling' began to make their appearance and threatened to bring about the very event that was dreaded.

The inflationary pressure in 1947 did not come so much from a quicker increase in the volume of the currency. In fact it was much slower than in the previous year. The note circulation which had increased from 4,889 million sch. in June 1946 to 5,656 million sch. in December, climbed only to 5,938 million sch. in March 1947, from which level it fell again to 5,547 million sch. in June. Only in the second half of the year was there a sharp upward turn which brought the notes in circulation to 6,219 million sch. at the end of October.

But the rising prices in 1946, distrust in the durability of the provisional currency regulations of 1945, the urgent need to buy in the high-priced black market led to strong demands from individuals and firms for the transfer of sums from blocked to free accounts and greatly accelerated the velocity of circulation. In the first ten months of 1947 [1] 438 million sch. were released from blocked accounts and 743 million sch. were withdrawn from free saving accounts. Though a buoyant revenue, which greatly exceeded the expected amount,[2] enabled the government to cover its ordinary and extraordinary expenditure and thus to avoid inflationary financing, a growing credit volume of the banks, which rose from 1,870 million sch. at the end of 1946 to 2,193 million sch. at the end of September 1947, contributed further to the inflationary forces.

This release of money hoards so far unused and the rising

[1] November was already influenced by the promulgation of the details of the forthcoming currency reform and has therefore to be left out of consideration when the events leading up to the currency reform are dealt with.

[2] This was partly due to the expansion in employment and production, but partly to the great influx of tax-debt payments before the currency reform. About the latter, see below, p. 50.

velocity of circulation multiplied the pressure on prices that had existed before. Applications for price and wage increases followed each other in quick succession and put a greater strain on the official control mechanism than it could bear. More and more the system of individual price control based on cost analysis crumbled away and general price increases first in industry and later also in agriculture threatened to develop into a general price and wage avalanche. The cost-of-living sub-index on clothing, which had risen by 17 per cent between April and December 1946, rose by 131 per cent between December 1946 and July 1947. For the total index the corresponding rises had been 26 per cent and 81 per cent respectively. Only wage-rates, which had advanced rather steeply towards the end of 1946, thus achieving a December index 38 per cent above the April index, developed at a slower rate, gaining till July 1947 33 per cent on the December level. With this slowing down they had fallen behind the rising cost of living which in July stood at 261 (April 1945 = 100), while wage-rates stood at 210.

The inflationary pressure did not affect official prices only. Black market prices, too, which owing to slowly improving supplies and the absorption of small savings had fallen all through 1946, began to show an upward tendency, though the gap between official and black market prices continued to decline.

When at the beginning of harvest time the peasants demanded a sharp advance in agricultural prices in order to close the scissors that had opened between prices of industrial and farm products,[1] it became clear that such a step would greatly accelerate the inflationary advance. A decisive cutting down of the volume of money or much more effective economic control could have prevented it. But economic control had already been allowed to lose too much of its grip to be effective at short notice, and on the whether, when, and how of a currency reform neither the Government nor the representative economic bodies were agreed.

In the event it was decided to prevent a chaotic run-away inflation by a quickly improvised measure, a so-called price-

---

[1] This gap between agricultural and industrial prices was partly relieved by the high prices obtained for foodstuffs in the black market.

wage agreement (later called the First Price-Wage Agreement, as a second and third one followed in 1948 and 1949), based on a compromise reached between the Chambers of Labour, Industry, and Agriculture in August 1947. Though put forward as a measure to prevent inflation it was in reality an attempt to anticipate the next inflationary steps in an organized fashion with a hope of stabilizing the wage-price structure at a higher level.

The essential idea of the First Price-Wage Agreement was to advance wages and prices, but at different rates so as to even out some of the disequilibria that had arisen in the official price structure. Thus the rates of public utilities, which had long remained at a very low level, were advanced most, from 50 per cent for passenger railway fares to over 100 per cent for postal services. Agricultural prices, too, were allowed to rise considerably—on an average by 58 per cent. These prices were fixed at this higher level and the effect of this on the cost-of-living index was calculated. It was then decided to raise wages and salaries so as to cover most though not necessarily the whole of the resulting rise in the cost of living.[1] Industrial prices were not so rigidly determined but certain rules were laid down as to how the new basic prices and wages should be taken into account for the fixing of new prices. These, it was hoped, would rise less than the agricultural prices. The whole agreement was laid down for three months in the first instance, and the trade unions were given the right to demand higher wages at any time should the cost-of-living index exceed the index of wage rates by more than 10 per cent. When the three months had elapsed the excess was in fact 14½ per cent. But the General Council of the Trade Unions (*Gewerkschaftsbund*) agreed to continue the agreement, which remained in force till September 1948.

The immediate effect of the Price-Wage Agreement was, as has been mentioned before, to raise prices and wages all round. In September the cost of living stood 31 per cent

---

[1] The wage increases were not of a uniform percentage, but favoured low incomes against big ones, and wages against salaries. In this way the Price-Wage Agreement continued the tendency towards a levelling of non-profit incomes that characterized the war and post-war period. This tendency was to some extent justified by the necessity to secure the minimum needs of the lower income groups in the face of a generally low standard of living. But it had a harmful effect by lowering the incentive to industrial mobility.

above the July figure (at 342 per cent of April 1945) and net wage-rates were 46 per cent above the July level (305 per cent of April 1945). This upward revision of the whole price structure 'by order' did not bring about an equilibrium. Neither did it remove all the unbalanced relationships in the official price and wage structure, nor 'take up' the huge money and credit volume; in September black market food prices were still nineteen times the official prices (they had stood at thirty-three times the official prices in June). But the Agreement succeeded in preventing the continuation of the quick upward movement in prices and wages that had set in towards the middle of 1947. As is usually the case when a government is reluctant to apply controls, the stabilization of wages was more successful than that of prices. In fact, wage rates remained stable at the level reached in September until July 1948.[1] Prices, however, continued to rise, though much more slowly than before. In November, the cost-of-living index stood 3·7 per cent above the September level. In any case, the Price-Wage Agreement had provided a breathing space which permitted the preparation of the second currency reform calculated to round off the unfinished steps of the first reform of December 1945.

THE INFLATIONARY DEVELOPMENT IN 1947

	Notes in circulation	Free saving deposits	Net wage-rates*	Cost of living*	Black-market food prices*
	(mill. sch.)		(April 1945 = 100)		(Aug. 1945=100)
Jan.	5,722	3,358	164	145	26
Feb.	5,853	3,293	164	154	23
March	5,938	3,193	164	166	22
April	5,896	3,138	174	169	23
May	5,707	3,072	180	188	22
June	5,547	3,015	204	189	24
July	5,595	2,899	210	261	24
Aug.	5,874	2,806	306	301	26
Sept.	6,099	2,723	305	342	27
Oct.	6,219	2,614	305	350	27
Nov.	4,809†	2,573	305	355	25
Dec.	—‡	953	305	357	32

* These index numbers apply to Vienna. The wage rates are net of income tax and social security payments.

† This reduction is due to the heavy influx of cash into the National Bank after the terms of the currency reform had become known. See below, p. 50.

‡ In view of the currency reform no returns were given for the end of December.

---

[1] Net *earnings* rose during this period, as with the improvement in equipment and raw material supplies longer hours and overtime were worked, and higher productivity increased incomes where payments were on the basis of results.

That such a currency reform would have to come sooner or later was commonly accepted. But there had been widespread disagreement as to whether it should await more settled economic and political conditions, and how the burdens, which would necessarily accompany it, should be distributed. Now, however, the majority of the Government felt that the precarious stability achieved by the Price-Wage Agreement would not last long if it were not soon followed by a measure that would remove, or at least reduce the large surplus volume of money. Moreover, rumours of an imminent currency reform and half-hearted official denials had so multiplied in 1947 that the consequent disquiet among wide circles of the population had a harmful effect on business life.

One of the special difficulties of a currency reform in Austria lay in the provisions of the Austrian occupation statute. The success of a currency reform is largely dependent on its sudden introduction, which prevents people from finding loopholes and means of evasion, and which secures a quick and smooth change-over to the new situation. The occupation statute, however, required that every Austrian law should only become valid thirty-one days after its promulgation by Parliament, and provided that not all four occupation Powers objected to it, in which case the law should not come into force at all.[1] It is not unlikely that in the special case of the currency reform careful negotiations with the occupation Powers could have secured an exception to this rule which would have allowed the immediate enforcement of the relevant legislation. For negotiations that were carried on after the currency laws had been passed by Parliament on 19 November did in fact result in a shortening of the stipulated thirty-one days' period so that the laws came into force on 10 December.

As it was, however, a period of twenty-one days elapsed during which everyone knew the terms of the currency reform, and in particular that on 10 December he would have to exchange part of his cash at the rate of three old schillings to one new schilling. The effects of such a state of affairs can be imagined. They not only led to the most topsy-turvy three weeks imaginable, but also reduced the effectiveness of the

---

[1] In the case of laws changing the Constitution the objection of one occupation Power suffices to prevent the law from becoming valid.

currency reform. A purchasing fever set in, with everybody trying to buy as much as he could with the old currency while sellers were of course not at all keen to part with their goods against money that would lose two-thirds of its value within a few days. Shops kept closed as much as they could in spite of Government orders to the contrary, or hid away their high-quality goods while selling their oldest surplus commodities at fantastic prices. Only in the vital field of rationed foodstuffs was a break-down of normal sales prevented by promising the producers and traders concerned an exchange of their receipts in this transition period into new schillings at the rate of one for one.

Not less strange was the picture that unfolded itself in the field of debtor-creditor relationships. Debtors hastened to pay off their debts in old schillings, very often well in advance of the date they were due, while creditors looked desperately for legal clauses which would enable them to refuse payment at that particular time. Tax payments, which in Austria came in, if anything, slower than in many other countries, poured into the Treasury and a special announcement had to be made that the numerous advance tax payments for 1948 could not be accepted. This accumulation of debt repayment led to a flow of cash into the banks and from there to the National Bank so that the notes in circulation sank rapidly from 6·2 milliard sch. on 7 November to 2·8 milliard sch. on 10 December while the deposits at the National Bank [1] jumped up from 2·8 milliard sch. to 6·2 milliard sch. This repayment of tax debt and credits reduced the effectiveness of the currency reform because, while the citizens' money was to be exchanged at the rate of 3 : 1, the State's money was exchanged at $1\frac{1}{3}$: 1 and the reserves of the banks at the National Bank were not reduced at all. [2] In addition to this factor which kept the post-reform circulation at a higher level than was originally anticipated the transition period had also encouraged illegal machinations to evade some of the regulations of the currency reform. But though they made a lot of difference to individual

---

[1] Not counting the blocked accounts.

[2] This was done in order to increase the liquidity of the banks. When, however, the reserves of the banks increased so suddenly in the days before the enforcement of the currency reform it was decided to block part of the reserves in order to prevent too rapid a credit expansion after the reform.

fortunes it is unlikely that they had important quantitative effects on the outcome of the reform.

On 10 December this strange transition period came to an end, and the currency legislation was put into effect. Its main provisions were: (1) An exchange of notes at the rate of 1 : 1 for 150 sch.[1] per head, and 3 : 1 for the remaining notes; (2) the eradication without compensation of all blocked accounts with the exception of accounts belonging to persons in difficult social conditions who were allowed to keep amounts up to 2,500–3,500 sch. which could be withdrawn in monthly instalments of 250–350 sch.; (3) the conversion of partly available accounts into 2 per cent government securities (with a maximum life of fifteen years) which could be used as means of payment for the capital levy which was to follow later; [2] (4) the preservation of the full value of all free accounts,[3] of which, however, so far as they exceeded 1,000 sch. half was to be blocked for half a year and a quarter for three-quarters of a year.

There is no doubt that these measures, while not yet establishing quite normal and stable monetary foundations, greatly reduced the inflationary pressure that had constantly hung over the country's economic life and had often exerted a distorting influence. The note circulation which had stood at 6·2 milliard sch. on 7 November fell to 1·6 milliard sch. immediately after the currency reform, while the free accounts at the National Bank (the reserves of the commercial banks and public funds) rose from 2·8 milliard sch. to 4 milliard sch. in view of debt repayment. If we add these two items we obtain the monetary and credit basis of the economy: it can be seen that it fell from 9 milliard sch. to 5·6 milliard sch. After the currency reform the flow of money to the banks and to the National Bank was of course reversed, and at the end of January 1948 the free accounts at the National Bank were

[1] Approximately one week's wage.

[2] See below. The very slow progress made in applying this capital levy (which reduces the demand for these securities) and the urgent demand for money on the part of some of these security owners (for whom these securities represent their small savings) has brought it about that the price of these securities—since they were admitted for dealings in the Stock Exchange in February 1949—has fluctuated between 50 sch. and 66 sch. for a nominal value of 100 sch. In the first half of 1950 they fell to 40 sch.

[3] These were part of the deposits created between June 1945 and December 1945 and all the deposits created between December 1945 and 12 November 1947.

down to 2 milliard sch. and the note circulation up to 3·7 milliard sch. But their sum was still 5·7 milliard sch.; there had been no credit expansion on the part of the Government or the banks yet.

In addition to this reduction in the means of circulation the fate of 7·9 milliard sch. of blocked accounts at the commercial banks and saving banks was finally settled by removing them altogether.[1]

While the currency reform thus carried out comparatively successfully a necessary operation—though opinions were divided whether the cut should have been deeper or more lenient—it failed to achieve a socially just distribution of the burden. The 1 : 1 exchange for 150 sch. for every person, and the modest release of blocked saving accounts for those absolutely dependent on them, were the only socially sympathetic considerations entering the currency reform. But many had hoped that this reform would be used to treat differentially the huge fortunes amassed during the war and on the post-war black market, and the small savings from many, many years of hard work. Moreover, the exclusive attention given to monetary wealth penalized those decent savers who had patiently followed the Government's advice to trust the currency, while the speculators and black marketeers who had been quick in turning their monetary gains into real estate, raw materials, carpets, fur coats, and what not, escaped the consequences of the currency reform.

It is true that at the time the currency legislation was passed it was promised that very soon—in January 1948—a levy on capital and capital gains would follow which would remove just these social injustices by taxing non-monetary wealth and aiming particularly at abnormal war and post-war gains. In actual fact, however, it took several months before this legislation reached Parliament and then it was much more restricted than was to have been expected after the clear-cut measures of the currency reform. Payments under the

[1] At the National Bank the system of blocked accounts continued to exist, firstly because part of the commercial banks' deposits were temporarily blocked (most of which were released in the first half of 1948), and secondly because the schilling receipts for goods received under Unrra and American interim aid and later Marshall Aid had to be deposited in a special blocked account (the so-called counterpart fund) at the National Bank which can only be used by the Government after obtaining the consent of the Unrra or E.R.P. authorities.

capital levy, for instance, can under certain circumstances be spread over more than twenty years. Even this mild form of capital levy had, however, still not been put into action in the autumn of 1949.[1] This delay in itself, in a period of rising prices, must reduce further the real return of the levy. In fact, there can be little doubt that this capital levy, if it ever is paid, will turn out just as much a mere formality as did a similar measure after the First World War. At best it will result in a small addition to income tax at a time when it is likely to be reduced from its present level in any case.

1948-9: TOWARDS A FREE MARKET ECONOMY

The currency reform had the effect which is usually associated with the restoration of more normal monetary conditions. Money became once again a scarce and desired object. Goods which before had vanished under the counter began to appear in the shop windows. The supply of labour increased with income opportunities on the black market deteriorating and with wives and other members of the family looking for additional earnings in order to increase a small family income which no longer could be supplemented from savings. The shortage of cash caused a sharp decline in black market prices; food prices on the black market fell between October 1947 and May 1948 by 68 per cent and exchange rates in the black market by 61 per cent. Even official prices felt to a slight extent the impact of the reduced purchasing power and prices of some of the industrial and less essential goods which had enjoyed easy boom conditions in the period of floating quantities of consumers' surplus money had to be reduced. The cost-of-living index, which continued to climb after the currency reform to a level of 368 (April 1945 = 100) in March 1948, fell gradually to 357, the level of December 1947, in September. Some branches of economic activity, which had easily expanded in the inflationary period, such as the publishing trade and the entertainments industry, found themselves in serious straits with people having to economize severely to buy the necessities of life. Total employment

[1] Though advance payments carrying with them rebates up to 30 per cent were invited by the Treasury.

continued to increase slowly, but the labour market had grown tighter and found it difficult to absorb the 'hidden reserves' which were now coming forth in search of jobs. Unemployment rose from a monthly average of 52,839 persons in 1947 to 61,356 in the second half of 1948 and 113,228 in the first half of 1949. At the same time vacancies reported to the labour exchanges—most of them offering agricultural employment—which had stood at 102,810 on the 1947 average had come down to 35,023 and 39,381 in the second half of 1948 and the first half of 1949 respectively.

With these developments taking place the main problem facing the Government in the field of monetary policy after the currency reform was to steer a course which would avoid both a deflationary shrinkage of economic activity and an inflationary expansion that could wreck what had been achieved by the currency reform and would further shake the confidence of a public too experienced in the meaning of inflation. This task of finding a proper monetary policy was rendered more difficult by the aim of the Government to reduce economic interventionism as quickly as possible and to return to an economy largely directed by 'the forces of the market'. This meant that the Government began to dispense with those non-monetary tools of economic policy, like price control, rationing, controls over the deployment of labour and materials, which, when used judiciously, can help to neutralize undesired effects of monetary and credit policies. This made the proper choice of a 'correct' monetary policy even more decisive.

The fear that the currency reform would lead straight into a deflationary crisis proved incorrect. After a certain scarcity of money had made itself felt in the first months after the reform, an expansion of money and credit took place which continued the upward movement that had existed before December 1947, though on a much milder scale.

Factors making for expansion which came automatically into force were the release of a limited number of blocked accounts for needy persons and the opening of those parts of the free over-1,000 sch. accounts which had been provisionally frozen, in June and September 1948. These additions to monetary circulation, which had already been taken into account when the currency reform was shaped, probably did not surpass that measure of expansion that was justified by the growing production and productivity. This seemed the more true as the transfer of the proceeds from the sale of relief goods (Unrra, American interim aid, E.R.P.) to a blocked account in the National Bank (which at the beginning of 1948 contained 1½ milliard sch.) led to a withdrawal of some 150 million sch. every month in 1948 and 250 million sch. in 1949 [1] from active circulation, which could have produced a deflationary effect. In fact, however, this deflationary effect was largely neutralized by repeated releases from this counterpart fund. With the consent of the American authorities (since summer 1948 the E.C.A. authorities) about 1·3 milliard sch. were released in 1948 and a further 550 million sch. till August 1949 to cover food subsidies, extraordinary Government expenditure, housing, and various investment projects. Further, 850 million sch. were withdrawn from circulation by using them for reducing the Government's debt to the National Bank.

In addition to these releases from blocked accounts there was a remarkable credit expansion by the banks. In spite of a high rate of interest—the rate for short-term credits being as high as 8½ per cent—credits outstanding at the commercial banks increased from 2,146 million sch. at the end of 1947 to 4,915 million sch. in March 1949. This expansion was partly based on the release of the banks' blocked accounts in the National Bank and a growing re-discount of treasury bills at the National Bank, partly, however, by a rapid running down of the banks' liquidity reserves. The ratio of the banks' free accounts at the National Bank to their total current and saving deposits fell from 30·9 per cent in January 1948 and 15·1 per cent in June 1948 to 5·5 per cent in mid-1949.

Finally, an unbalanced budget burdened by high current and investment expenditure, the cost of occupation and displaced persons, and a heavy deficit of the State railways contributed further to an expansionary monetary development. [2]

[1] The sharp rise in proceeds in 1949 is only partly due to increased relief shipments ; it largely reflects the higher internal prices at which relief goods were sold.

[2] Part of the public deficit, particularly as far as extraordinary (investment) expenditure is concerned, was financed by sums released from the blocked counterpart fund. This part had, therefore, no *additional* expansionist effect to that mentioned earlier in connexion with the counterpart fund.

All these factors, releases from various blocked accounts, credit expansion, budget deficit, led to a quick expansion in currency circulation. The note circulation, which had stood at 3,687 million sch. at the end of January 1948, rose steadily to 5,877 million sch. in April 1949, whence it fell to a slightly lower level in the summer months. Such an expansion far surpassed the increased monetary needs of an expanding volume of production and transactions. Some of the growth in note circulation went into increased cash holdings to which firms and individuals returned once the worst inflation fears were removed and some was absorbed by a very slowly increasing volume of savings. Saving deposits increased from 958 million sch. at the end of January 1948 to 1,562 million sch. in June 1949.[1]

But the rest of the expansion exerted an upward pressure on prices and wages, which for some time could be checked by sticking to the terms of the First Price-Wage Agreement, but which became more and more irresistible as time went on. This pressure was met by returning to the method of wholesale upward revisions of the entire price-wage structure which had first been applied in the inflation—the grave days of the late summer 1947. Thus the Second Price-Wage Agreement of September 1948 and the Third Price-Wage Agreement of May 1949 were born. And while each had to serve the purpose of bringing the value of total transactions more into line with an overgrown monetary and credit volume, with a hope of subsequent stabilization, an attempt was also made to clear up some economic difficulties or contradictions that had crept in.

Thus the Second Price-Wage Agreement had to pave the way for the abolition of food subsidies, which the Government wanted to remove in order to relieve its budget and particularly in order to return to a free market mechanism.[2] As a first step

---

[1] The smallness of this sum can be gauged from the fact that in 1937, with a note circulation less than a sixth of the present level, saving deposits amounted to 2,348 million sch.

[2] For reasons difficult to understand the Government and most of the Austrian economic press have taken it for granted that price subsidies are something 'unhealthy' which should be removed as quickly as possible. No such attitude was taken, however, with respect to the numerous and heavy indirect taxes which are nothing but negative subsidies. (Indirect taxes are, of course, a welcome revenue for the exchequer while subsidies are not. But from a general economic point of view both are equivalent 'interventions' into the 'free market mechanism'.)

In fact, a strong case could have been made in Austria for a continuation of food subsidies in view of the very precarious living standards in the lowest income brackets.

the subsidies for meat and milk products were removed. This meant a rise in the cost-of-living sub-index for foodstuffs from 348 to 465, and of the total index from 357 to 423. To compensate this rise in prices and to secure minimum standards of living for the lower-income groups and larger families, this increase in food prices was coupled with an increase in wages and salaries by 6 per cent, a flat-rate food bonus of 34 sch. a month per employee to be paid by the employers, and a family allowance of 23 sch. a month per child to be paid by the State. These measures raised the index of net wages for a wage-earner with two children from 308 to 375. Industrial prices, which became more and more subject to the laws of the 'grey market' (the de-controlled market where prices were lower than in the former black market but well above the former controlled prices for rationed goods), were once again left to increase slowly.

Far more complicated than the First and Second Price-Wage Agreements was the more comprehensive third one. This was initiated by a threatening budget deficit for 1949 about three to four times the size of that of 1948. This was partly due to disappointing revenue from some taxes, in particular from the tobacco tax which suffered from illegally imported American and Balkan cigarettes (sold tax-free), and a heavy deficit on the railways. Partly, however, it was the consequence of an over-sized extraordinary budget [1] and a badly estimated ordinary budget which was manipulated to show a surplus by transferring some items of current expenditure to the extraordinary account. In order to prevent this deficit from materializing, the rates for public services and the railways were drastically increased and new taxes on income and capital introduced which fell particularly heavily on medium incomes. The purchase tax was also increased. At the same time the remaining subsidies for coal and grain were abolished. The consequent rise in prices should have been partly covered by a rise in wages and salaries consisting of a flat-rate addition of 0·30 sch. per hour or 60 sch. per month to take the place of the former food bonus, and a 4½ per cent rise of the wage thus arrived at, as well as an increase of the

---

[1] Built on hopes of E.C.A. authorizations for the use of the blocked counterpart fund, which did not fully materialize.

children's allowances from 23 sch. to 37 sch. Social insurance contributions were also increased to fill the one serious gap in Austria's otherwise advanced social security legislation: to introduce old-age pensions for workers. Industry was permitted to pass on the increased costs in higher prices but the (pious) hope was expressed that firms would try to absorb some of the increases by reducing profits. In fact, important industrial prices, such as those for iron, textiles, and paper, did show a marked rise, while price increases for commodities in elastic demand were effectively checked by the fall in purchasing power. For the new Price-Wage Agreement had raised the cost-of-living index by 19 per cent, from 427 to 508, but had raised the *net* wage of a Viennese worker with two children by only 10 per cent, from 377 to 413.

The introduction of the price-wage agreements has thus not prevented the upward movement of prices and wages fostered by monetary and credit expansion, but has concentrated it into short periods of sudden jerks with fairly stable periods in between. But fascinating though the idea of the First Price-Wage Agreement perhaps was as one orderly upward revision to prevent a sudden chaotic run-away, the value of the subsequent agreements must be viewed with much greater scepticism. First, the mere fact that an agreement heralded to bring about stabilization had to be followed by other similarly drastic measures reduces the psychological value which may be claimed for such a general 'spring cleaning'. Then, with the growth and diversification which Austria's economic life had achieved by 1948, the possibilities of securing major economic adjustments in a basically uncontrolled economy by single and global acts were bound to be small; what was necessary were numerous readjustments in *relative* prices and wages which could not possibly be dealt with in a few weeks' negotiations. And finally, with the growing decontrol of production, prices, and distribution the price-wage agreements have meant more and more the imposition of a wage-stop without a corresponding price-stop, except for limited quantities of the bare essentials of food. It is unlikely that such a one-sided application of economic control will be accepted for long by the trade unions.

THE MONETARY DEVELOPMENT IN 1948-9

	Notes in circulation	Outstanding bank credits (million sch.)	Saving deposits	Cost of living* (April 1945	Net wages*† = 100)
1948					
Jan. . .	3,687		958	360	305
Feb. . .	3,874		971	360	305
Mar. .	3,994	2,712	1,119	368	305
Apr. .	4,137		1,184	364	305
May	4,265		1,227	364	305
June .	4,475	3,044	1,223	362	305
July .	4,737		1,235	358	308
Aug. .	4,914		1,243	358	308
Sept. .	5,132	3,436	1,228	357	308
Oct. .	5,299		1,247	423	375
Nov. .	5,388		1,248	431	377
Dec. .	5,635	4,206	1,272	433	377
1949					
Jan. .	5,669		1,332	435	377
Feb. .	5,816		1,396	431	377
Mar. .	5,833	4,915	1,461	429	377
Apr. .	5,877		1,511	428	377
May	5,765		1,552	427	377
June .	5,797	5,477	1,562	508	413
July .	5,996		1,573	509	417

* In Vienna.
† Wage income minus wage tax and social security payments.

The fact that the currency reform was followed by an inflationary rather than a deflationary tendency meant that its occasional restricting effects could not hold up the continuation of the general increase in production. It also meant that with prices and profits developing faster than wages the stimulus towards investment continued at a high rate. The index of production continued to rise, apart from seasonal set-backs, and reached the 1937 level in June 1948. In the months March-May 1949 it stood 18 per cent above that level. But the production of investment materials and goods had increased between January 1948 and May 1949 by 75 per cent, reaching 171 per cent of 1937, while the consumer goods industries grew by 68 per cent to only 90 per cent of 1937.

Foreign trade also continued its upward course though it could not reach such favourable results as production, when compared with pre-war standards. The volume of exports almost doubled between the first quarter of 1948 and the first quarter of 1949, but even so it only reached two-thirds of the 1937 volume (already a small one) at the latter period.

The expansion of foreign trade, in spite of a rise in prices which brought most Austrian export prices when valued at the official exchange-rate of 40 sch. to the £ well above world prices, was only possible by continuing the system of individual barter deals and acquiescing in a *de facto* devaluation of the schilling by permitting the sale of part of the export proceeds to importers at higher schilling rates. This system has become formally established through Austria following the devaluation of the other countries rather belatedly on 22 November 1949. The 'basic exchange rate' was devalued to the same extent as the pound sterling. Forty per cent of the export proceeds have to be sold to the National Bank at this rate. The remaining 60 per cent the exporter can use himself or can sell through the National Bank to importers at a 'premium rate' which, though variable in principle, has, to begin with, been pegged at 72 sch. to the £. The exporter thus obtains for his total revenue an 'effective rate' of 59·20 sch. to the £. Imports have been classified into three groups according to importance, for which foreign exchange is sold either at the basic, the effective, or the premium rate. A limited number of vital foodstuffs obtained under E.R.P. are to be kept at the pre-devaluation rate for some time in order to prevent a marked rise in the cost of living.

Although this somewhat complicated looking devaluation method largely follows the pattern that had evolved in practice, certain changes will result in the composition and perhaps in the volume of exports and imports, because of the shifts in a number of price relationships.

These methods were coupled with an increasing relaxation in the controls over exports and imports. The consequence was a growing direction of exports towards the more profitable barter deals (*Kompensationsgeschäfte*), in particular with Italy (the only country with which trade has been arranged almost exclusively on a barter basis).[1] To Italy timber and other important products have been exported, often compensated by oranges, lemons, and other goods, which do not obtain

[1] Italy's share in total exports has grown from 16 per cent in 1947 and 17 per cent in 1948 to 22 per cent in the first six months of 1949. She is now Austria's most important export partner and second in imports only to Germany (whence large E.R.P. coal imports are obtained). Beginning with July 1950 the trade with Italy was put on a clearing basis.

high priority in international trade negotiations nowadays, but could fetch high prices in the Austrian market, thus securing a better return to the exporter than exports to hard currency areas.[1]

PRODUCTION, EMPLOYMENT, AND FOREIGN TRADE, 1948-9

	Index of production	Production of means of production	Production of consumer goods	Employed persons	Unemployed persons	Imports*	Exports	Imports*	Exports
		(1937=100)		(000 omitted)		(million sch.)		1937=100	
1948									
Jan.	74	98	53	1,849·6	50·1	167·0	87·3	} 37	36
Feb.	75	98	56	1,854·9	48·4	175·6	106·9		
Mar.	83	111	60	1,866·4	46·7	200·6	141·9		
April	87	120	60	1,889·6	45·9	206·6	144·3	} 44	50
May	90	125	61	1,904·1	47·4	178·8	163·5		
June	101	141	69	1,911·8	49·0	211·6	161·2		
July	100	145	63	1,916·5	51·7	222·3	173·8	} 52	56
Aug.	104	149	67	1,929·2	52·1	222·5	159·3		
Sept.	104	144	71	1,933·4	51·9	231·6	183·1		
Oct.	103	141	72	1,931·8	55·7	219·5	191·1	} 56	65
Nov.	101	137	72	1,926·6	63·1	238·0	219·0		
Dec.	101	137	71	1,877·9	93·7	328·1	252·3		
1949									
Jan.	94	127	68	1,842·2	131·0	265·5	223·4	} 65	68
Feb.	96	126	71	1,833·1	138·7	293·6	234·7		
Mar.	112	146	86	1,847·1	130·2	364·9	286·8		
April	116	153	85	1,884·9	108·0	338·7	258·3		
May	126	171	90	1,915·2	90·8	341·0	291·3		
June	128	169	94	1,933·3	80·6	391·4	288·9		

* Excluding the larger part of the relief imports.

The insufficient recovery of foreign trade and the use of part of the exports to pay for inessential imports has resulted in a continued dependence of Austria on foreign help. Decisive quantities of basic requirements, such as food, agricultural

[1] The profits obtained by such barter deals rest on the very different price differentials (let us say between timber and oranges) in the two countries and a restriction system which prevents the assimilation of relative prices in both countries. This system often leads to strange results. Thus Italian importers who had obtained Austrian timber at the low price of the oranges which they sent in exchange, were able to re-sell this timber below Austrian prices in Middle Eastern markets.

supplies, coal, and various raw materials were obtained from American interim aid and E.R.P. deliveries. The balance-of-payments deficit in 1948 was probably close on 3 milliard sch., a sum which corresponds approximately to the amount of 2,800 million sch. ($280 million) that was allocated to Austria for the first Marshall-Plan year (April 1948–March 1949).[1] For the second Marshall year the Austrian Government has again asked for an allocation of that size.[2]

While production and foreign trade thus continued the growth that had begun in 1945 and 1946, a decisive turn for the better was experienced in the field of agriculture where the set-backs of 1946 and 1947 were replaced by average harvests which in 1949 for the first time pointed towards a return to pre-war conditions.[3] The bread-grain harvest brought in 558,000 tons in 1948 and 726,000 tons in 1949. This latter figure represents 83 per cent of the 1937 harvest and 75 per cent of the 1934-8 average. In fact, the 1949 yields per hectare —1·8 tons of wheat and 1·7 tons of rye—thanks to very favourable weather conditions and to a greatly improved supply of fertilizers, were higher than before the war. Only the reduced area under cultivation has caused the smaller harvest result. But if the planned expansion in the area under cultivation is fulfilled [4] in the coming years and the weather is not too adverse, the Ministry of Agriculture target, to recapture the pre-war agricultural output by 1952, may be reached or even overreached.

[1] The total of foreign help obtained by Austria from the end of the war till the beginning of Marshall Aid has been estimated at $560 million. This is, however, a rough estimate combining dollar values of various purchasing powers and goods ranging from urgent necessities to comparatively unimportant war surplus goods.

[2] In fact, the second-year Marshall Aid has been cut down (direct aid plus drawing rights) to $252 million.

[3] It must be pointed out, however, that some of the advances in agriculture, production, and foreign trade since the currency reform are more statistical than real, as with the receding importance of the black market the inducement to conceal part of the production results has been reduced.

[4] In 1948 the planned figures were not quite reached.

III

CONCLUSIONS

The Transition from Post-War Adjustment to Long-Term Solutions

THE four years of post-war development in Austria of which a short description has been given, can, in one way, be regarded as the period of immediate post-war adjustment. That is, if we have to think in periods—and it seems a helpful device—it may be set aside as a period in itself. Not that in these four years all the detrimental actions and omissions of the war period had been overcome, or that Austria found a basis for a smoothly functioning, 'normal' peace-time economy (whatever that may mean in the light of the past thirty years' experience). On the contrary, in 1949 there were still many problems urgently awaiting solution. But many of them are closely connected with those of other European countries and are not specifically Austrian, while all of them may make their influence felt for many years to come. This is shown by the obstinacy with which these problems recur, and by the experience of the 1918-39 period, which throughout was disturbed by influences and disequilibria which, if not generated by the First World War, had been greatly intensified by it. If the effects of the changes brought about directly or indirectly by the Second World War during *all* the coming years were to be included in the post-war period the meaning of this term would have to be stretched far beyond any reasonable interpretation. Thus it seems justified to regard the period of 1945-9, in which production has recovered to a remarkable extent, agriculture has found a way towards a healthy basis, and the chaos of 1945 has given way to a closely interlocking economic system, as the period of intermediate post-war transition. And we have a right to regard the problems still in existence as questions which may, or may not, retain a

63

deeper and long-term significance. To a short discussion of these wider problems we must now turn.[1]

THE UNBALANCED STRUCTURE OF INTERNAL DEMAND AND PRODUCTION PATTERNS

Austria, like so many other war-torn countries, has passed from war to peace production with remarkable speed. She has also undergone two currency reforms without experiencing such increases in unemployment as Western Germany, or such a set-back in production as Italy. But the apparent prosperity in Austria rests on rather precarious foundations, both internally and externally. In fact, the comparative smoothness of the development up till now is largely due to the fact that both in the field of production and in the monetary sphere the really serious readjustments have not yet been made.

The internal market has so far been largely dominated by an investment boom fed by a large pent-up demand for repairs and new equipment and an inflationary development with wages frequently lagging behind profits. This boom has relied to a large extent on the production of the same basic and heavy industries which provided the backbone of the war economy. This has greatly eased the transition so far. But the very unevenness in incomes which has supported the investment boom is showing signs of bringing it to an end. Investment is not carried on for its own sake, and as its fruits come on to the market the low purchasing power of the great mass of the consumers provides a check on their sale, and thus on further investment. Beginnings of such developments have made themselves felt ever since the currency reform of 1947.

If we neglect at present the possibilities in the field of exports, it is obvious that the very uneven development in the post-war production of investment materials and goods and consumer goods, to which frequent reference has been made, is bound to cause stresses which may easily develop into major economic dislocations. But the change-over to a more balanced relationship cannot be easy. It involves difficult

---

[1] There is one factor still (1950) influencing Austria which must be regarded as an immediate post-war problem : that is the occupation. Its termination will remove a serious burden on the budget and on the population.

technical and economic changes in the type and use of equipment and perhaps even more difficult social changes in the distribution of income. Neither of these problems has been properly analysed, still less has there been any attempt to tackle them. On the contrary, the international post-war shortage of basic products and investment goods as well as the inheritance of such industries from the war period have concentrated the Government's interest on the expansion of this sphere.[1] This must lead to an intensification of the threatening contradictions, unless stable export markets can be found for these products, which under the present circumstances is rather doubtful; or, in the opinion of some, unless a deliberate policy of long-range industrial development by extensive planning is adopted, which is not the avowed policy of the present Government. A third possibility making an adjustment unnecessary, i.e. a return to war or to an economy on a war footing, can be omitted as outside the scope of this study of the chances and problems of a peaceful recovery of Austria's economy. Given Austria's geographical position, any war or even any permanent atmosphere of war-like tension would dash all hopes of recovery for a long time.

Monetary Adjustment

The adjustment difficulties in the industrial structure which must be expected from such 'real' causes as unbalanced technical equipment and a strongly skewed income distribution may be further aggravated or even separately promoted by the need for monetary adjustment. The investment boom and the whole post-war prosperity has been based on a continuous inflationary upward trend. The currency reform of 1947 removed the worst inflationary pressure but did not stop a monetary and credit expansion. The continued control of wages and the prices of rationed food kept the upward movement in check. But it is clear that with the growing relaxation of controls the management of money and credit will have to become tighter if new price-wage agreements and currency

[1] To some extent these expansion schemes are without doubt justified. This applies particularly to the various hydro-electric schemes now under construction or planned which will lead to an immediate saving in coal import needs or are likely to find export markets.

reforms are not to shake still further the confidence of an inflation-minded public. This tightening of money and credit will have to be even more severe if the Government is intent, as it has declared from time to time, to return as soon as possible to a much freer regime in foreign trade. Comparing the average note circulation in the first half of 1949 of 5,793 million sch. and gold and foreign exchange reserves of only 166·1 million sch. with the position in 1937, when a note circulation of 909 million sch. was backed by gold and foreign exchange reserves of 364·3 million sch. (each time valued at the current official exchange rates), one can see that a freer and non-discriminatory foreign trade policy would require a depreciation of the schilling on such a scale that it would have to be accompanied by considerable deflationary measures if the subsequent rise in import prices was not to start a strong inflationary spiral.

But even if we make the probable assumption that the adjustment to the tenets of the Bretton Woods and Havana Charters will have to wait in view of the complicated international situation, the milder disinflationary methods which will have to be applied to maintain domestic monetary equilibrium are also likely to upset an industrial development that has been geared to inflationary injections. If it were only a question of a short and sharp stabilization crisis weeding out some of the inflationary mushrooms, such a disturbance could only be welcomed. But since the monetary adjustment will hit an economy with serious structural unbalances, the effects are likely to go deeper. A restriction of credit will hasten the end of the post-war investment demand and could start serious industrial and regional recessions which might easily develop into major unemployment. In fact, by rapidly reducing its economic control apparatus the Government has greatly narrowed the path that divides inflation from deflation. It has also, while giving an immediate stimulus to various economic activities, reduced its power to attack directly the structural problems of the economy.

This question of a reduced scope for a positive and direct attack on some of the existing disequilibria (rather than negative and indirect methods, like general regulations and monetary policy) also affects the problem of the budget deficit. The obvious way to cut down the deficit would be to reduce the large expenditure on salaries. Since civil service salaries are extremely low this could only be done by considerable dismissals. Without any positive scheme for the re-absorption of these dismissed civil servants this would, however, merely re-create that permanent middle-class unemployment which had such a depressing influence on Austria's economy in the inter-war years.[1] On the other hand, to continue deficit expenditure maintains the danger of inflation, while an increase in taxation seems hardly possible in view of the very high rate of taxation already in force.[2]

THE BALANCE-OF-PAYMENTS PROBLEM

Not less pressing than the problem of internal is that of external adjustment.[3] Austria shares with the other Marshall Plan members a balance-of-payments deficit. The basis of the problem is in many respects similar to that of the other countries and in these respects does not require any special analysis here.[4] But what makes it more serious is the extent to which it has grown. The $280 million Marshall Aid which Austria has received in the first Marshall year represents the highest figure per head of any Marshall country;[5] it is 400 million sch. ($40 million) more than were the Austrian exports in the same period. And the Austrian Government in its long-term report to the O.E.E.C. still foresees an uncovered, though smaller, balance-of-payments deficit for 1952.

The particular gravity of the Austrian balance-of-payments

[1] On the present problem of white-collar unemployment see above, p. 25.

[2] Quite a lot could, however, be done by fighting the very widespread habit of tax evasion. This arose partly because taxes were so high. But once acquired this habit has the tendency to stay. Thus it would not be sufficient to reduce taxes somewhat; enforcement would also have to be improved.

Since wage and salary earners have their tax deducted from their pay the question of fighting tax evasion is at the same time a question of the distribution of the tax burden and thus links up with the problem mentioned earlier of income distribution (if we think of net incomes).

[3] The two are, of course, closely connected. Thus an increased scope for the export of products of heavy industry would reduce the need for internal structural changes.

[4] See, for instance, U.N. Economic Commission for Europe, *A Survey of the Economic Situation and Prospects of Europe* and *Economic Survey of Europe in 1948* (Geneva, 1948 and 1949).

[5] In the second Marshall year the Netherlands tops the list with the largest per head allocation, with Austria taking the second place.

deficit is above all due to the late recovery in exports and the extremely low level from which they started. As a consequence the development of exports has not only lagged behind that of production but also behind that in most other countries. In the middle of 1949 their volume had only reached 70 per cent of the 1937 volume. But the increase in population and the existence of a state of full employment would today demand a much bigger volume of imports and therefore of exports than in 1937. If we assume the same level of agricultural production and the same standard of living as in 1937 [1] and take into account the deterioration in the terms of trade [2] and the likelihood of a prolonged reduction in revenue from the 'invisible' items (say, to half the level of 1937 when measured at constant prices), independence from external aid would demand an expansion of the export volume to about 155 per cent of the 1937 level,[3] or more than double the level achieved in 1949. Of course, the stabilization of the standard of living below the 1937 level, a favourable change in the terms of trade, a more self-sufficient economic structure, or an unexpected expansion in tourist and transit trade could reduce the required increase in exports. But the insufficiency of the present level is clearly indicated.

Yet Austria is beginning, like other exporting countries, to feel the increase in international competition and the tightening of world markets. The slackening of world trade expansion which has become apparent since the middle of 1948 has also begun to affect Austrian exports, but on a much more dangerously low level than in most other countries. There is still room for quick and important advances in certain directions; trade treaties with South American and other overseas countries have still to be concluded and will open up new trading opportunities. But in general the time when new contacts and business connexions could be easily established

---

[1] This is to say that a man employed today would have to get the same real wage as in 1937. Since in 1937 there was considerable unemployment, this assumption really involves a higher average standard of living than in 1937.

[2] In the first quarter of 1949 the index of export prices stood at 362 (1937 = 100) and the index of import prices at 393. (This is only a very rough index, derived from a comparison of volume and value indices of foreign trade.)

[3] It must be remembered that the 1937 foreign trade volume was already a greatly reduced one. In 1929, with trade flowing much freer but also with an agriculture satisfying a much smaller part of domestic needs, the volume of exports was 69 per cent above that of 1937.

has passed by, and in future the conquest of markets is bound to be a more difficult and slower affair.

In addition to the problem of the total level of exports, there exists a structural problem in foreign trade, just as in the case of domestic production and demand. The post-war expansion in exports has been largely an expansion in goods which meet the specific demands of international post-war reconstruction. The exports of pig-iron and scrap-iron are now considerably bigger than in any pre-war year and have reached the same importance as the timber exports which before the war were by far the most important raw material exported.[1] But welcome though these increased iron exports have been they exemplify two weak spots in the export structure which can also be noted in the case of other commodity groups. On the one hand, they show the shift in Austria's exports from manufactured goods to raw materials. Raw materials and semi-manufactured goods which accounted for 23 per cent of total exports in 1929 and 30 per cent in 1937,[2] increased their share from 24 per cent in 1947 and 32 per cent in 1948 to 42 per cent in the first five months of 1949. This change, which means a very serious danger for Austria's manufacturing industries, a reduced foreign exchange income for Austria's basic resources,[3] and a greater sensitivity to external business fluctuations, is partly due to the general European post-war trade policy, which tries to keep out imports of 'inessential' goods and which hits some of Austria's traditional export branches,[4] and partly to the fact that in Austria the earlier stages of production have maintained a greater competitive strength than the later stages.

[1] In 1937 the value of pig and scrap iron exports amounted only to 19 per cent of the timber exports.

[2] This was the highest percentage reached in the first Republic and was partly a consequence of raw material deliveries for the German, Italian, and Japanese war economies.

[3] Which, of course, bring in a greater revenue the greater the value added in production. Generally speaking, international trade and national income figures show a very close positive correlation between the percentage of manufactured goods in exports and national income per head. This does not, of course, imply any direct causal relationship between these two magnitudes; rather, they are both expressions of a high degree of industrialization. Nevertheless, a permanent shift from exports of final goods to raw materials would probably affect the industrial structure and import opportunities in such a way as to lower the standard of living.

[4] But, as the *Economic Survey of Europe in 1948* shows, Europe as a whole has, in spite of this policy, been able to maintain its position as an exporter of manufactured goods.

THE PROBLEM OF EAST-WEST TRADE

But part of the problem is connected with the changes in the geographical distribution of exports, which also links up with the second weak spot to be mentioned. Austria's exports are today more orientated to the West than they were before the war. In the first post-war years this development was fostered by the bad harvests in Eastern Europe and the general paucity of goods Austria had to offer for international exchange; but since then the picture has changed and it is more and more the political tension between East and West that is responsible for the diverted flow of trade. Exports to four important Central and Eastern European trade partners—Czechoslovakia, Hungary, Poland, and Yugoslavia—which had accounted for 33·6 per cent of all exports in 1929, 26·1 per cent in 1937,[1] and still 25·1 per cent in 1946 (when Czechoslovakia was, with Switzerland and Italy, one of the principal trading partners), dropped to 18·4 per cent in 1947 and 17·5 per cent in 1948, recovering slightly to 19·5 per cent in the first five months of 1949, largely because of increased exports to Yugoslavia.[2] Trade with Bulgaria had never played an important part in Austria's foreign trade; but exports to Roumania, which in 1937 had been greater than those to Great Britain or Switzerland, have fallen to a quite insignificant level, since Roumania is the only Eastern European country with which a trade treaty has still to be concluded. This was done in April 1950.

Now such a change in geographical distribution cannot but have serious repercussions on Austria's export structure. Europe's standards of industrial efficiency have long, for a variety of reasons, shown a falling tendency from West to East.

[1] As a consequence of the politically inspired, so-called 'Rome Protocols' of 1934, Austria's foreign trade was diverted from the countries of the 'Little Entente' to Hungary and Italy.

[2] When looking at these percentages it must be remembered that most of the exports going to Poland are in exchange for coal from Upper Silesia which before the war belonged to Germany. If this is taken into account the post-war decline in trade with the above-mentioned group of countries is even greater than the figures quoted in the text suggest.

The separate figures for Czechoslovakia may be of some interest in this context. Exports to Czechoslovakia were expressed as a percentage of total exports:

(January-May)

1929	1937	1946	1947	1948	1949
13·5	7·2	19·1	9·3	7·5	6·5

CONCLUSIONS

That has always meant that Austria, because of transport advantages and a better knowledge of the needs and usages in Eastern Europe, and also because of a greater readiness to accept the produce of these countries, could sell some of her finished goods there which would hardly prove competitive in Western Europe or overseas. While the changed demand pattern which planning has brought to these countries must mean a permanent closure for some of Austria's traditional exports to these areas,[1] prospects for other goods, as for instance for the products of the important engineering industry, would seem to have become brighter. But the export of these products to Eastern Europe is discouraged under the Marshall Plan, while Austria has only limited opportunities of selling them in the West.

While the rupture of East-West trade thus contributes to the present shift in Austria's exports from manufactured goods to raw materials and semi-manufactured goods it also threatens the stability of the present Austrian export and industrial structure. And this brings us to the second weak point in the present export development. It has already been pointed out that in the domestic market the investment goods industries have reached a relative size which can be easily supported under the special post-war investment boom conditions, but may give rise to serious adjustment difficulties at a later stage. Now, it seems that in the field of exports the situation is not unlike that in the domestic field. Here, too, exports have quickly expanded in the field of those raw materials and commodities which were urgently required in the international post-war reconstruction and investment boom. But this boom is now showing signs of dying down in several countries while production and international competition are quickly increasing. Austria, which in some of these commodities is a marginal high-cost producer, will feel the pinch just at a time when her domestic situation will also exert a depressing influence on the same industries. This combined pressure may well cause serious adjustment crises. Again, closer trade relations with the eastern planned economies, whose investment demand is likely to remain at a relatively high level for a long time to come, would ease the adjustment problem.

[1] For instance, certain textile goods.

THE OUTLOOK

The picture of Austria's problems as developed here may to some readers seem rather sombre or even pessimistic. Such a conclusion would, however, be unjustified. Problems are here to be solved. There is nothing in Austria's problems, severe though they are, which should make them appear as insoluble. Certainly, as they are tackled one by one new difficulties will arise and new ways will have to be discovered.

The main danger is not that these difficulties will prove insurmountable, but that the problems are not recognized in time. Even then they will, of course, not lead to a complete break-down of Austria's economy. Political economies abhor a vacuum. Problems get solved either by finding a solution to them or by default. The latter way also leads to some sort of 'equilibrium', but at the cost of untold and unnecessary human misery and perhaps the independence of the country. This was to some extent the fate of the first Austrian Republic where economic ills were partly not diagnosed in time, partly not courageously tackled.

To avoid repetition of these past mistakes will be the supreme task for wise statesmanship.

APPENDICES

Appendix I

Statistical Tables

I. PRODUCTION

| Year | Quarter | Index of production in mining and basic industries (1937 = 100) | GENERAL INDEX OF PRODUCTION | | |
			Total	Investment materials and goods (1937 = 100)	Consumer goods
1946	I	49			
	II	55			
	III	67			
	IV	62			
1947	I	51	43	59	30
	II	74	64	88	45
	III	79	68	96	45
	IV	77	69	93	50
1948	I	86	77	102	56
	II		93	129	64
	III	This index was discontinued after the first quarter of 1948	103	146	67
	IV		102	138	72
1949	I		101	133	75
	II		123	164	90
	III		126	174	88
	IV		—	—	—

II. EMPLOYMENT AND UNEMPLOYMENT

(ooo omitted)

Year	Quarter	Total number of health-insured employees*	Employees in industry and trade	Employees in agriculture	Unemployment†
1946	I	1,541·1	1,052·4	253·9	82·7
	II	1,687·4	1,209·3	272·1	79·6
	III	1,821·8	1,296·7	289·1	70·0
	IV	1,867·9	1,373·2	272·9	64·1
1947	I	1,819·2	1,357·3	263·0	71·7
	II	1,876·5	1,393·2	275·3	58·3
	III	1,901·3	1,408·6	282·5	40·9
	IV	1,888·8	1,413·6	263·0	40·5
1948	I	1,856·9	1,390·4	248·8	48·4
	II	1,901·8	1,426·6	257·0	47·4
	III	1,926·4	1,443·8	261·6	51·9
	IV	1,912·1	1,440·8	246·2	70·8
1949	I	1,840·8	1,384·3	233·9	133·3
	II	1,911·1	1,445·9	244·3	93·1
	III	1,954·3	1,482·3	249·8	74·0
	IV	1,936·2	1,477·4	234·2	99·9

* The total includes civil servants and employees of the Federal Railways who are not contained in the two sub-groups.

† Number of people who register at the labour exchanges. This contains a small number of people who only want short-period employment or change of employment, but excludes all those unemployed who look for jobs without registering with the labour exchange.

III. MONEY AND CREDIT
(in million sch.)

Year	Quarter	Notes in circulation	Credits outstanding at the commercial banks†	Free saving deposits
1946	I	3,892	—	—
	II	4,636	1,725	3,856
	III	5,126	1,812	3,734
	IV	5,331	1,870	3,498
1947	I	5,756	1,941	3,290
	II	5,717	2,012	3,075
	III	5,856	2,193	2,809
	IV	—*	2,146	2,047
1948	I	3,852	2,712	1,016
	II	4,292	3,044	1,211
	III	4,928	3,436	1,235
	IV	5,441	4,206	1,256
1949	I	5,773	4,915	1,396
	II	5,813	5,477	1,542
	III	5,923	6,238	1,577
	IV	5,559	7,007	1,643

* Because of the currency reform no figures were published for December 1947.
† The figures in this column are not quarterly averages but refer to the end of each quarter.

IV. PRICES AND WAGES

Year	Quarter	Wholesale prices* March 1938=100	Cost of living† April 1945=100	Net wages‡ April 1945=100
1946	I	—	—	—
	II	—	114	117
	III	—	123	130
	IV	—	140	145
1947	I	—	155	164
	II	—	182	186
	III	—	301	274
	IV	296	354	305
1948	I	300	362	305
	II	297	363	305
	III	299	358	308
	IV	356	429	376
1949	I	355	432	377
	II	385	455	389
	III	420	501	418
	IV	453	517	418

* Wholesale prices of foodstuffs, drink, and industrial raw materials and intermediate products.

† Cost of living in Vienna for a working-class household with two children on the basis of pre-war consumption habits and official prices for rationed goods.

‡ Wage-rate for workers in Vienna with two children net of taxes, social security, and trade union contributions, and including children's allowances. The index is a weighted average of skilled and unskilled, male and female wage-rates.

APPENDICES

V. FOREIGN TRADE

Year	Quarter	Imports*	Exports	Volume of Imports*	Exports
		(Mill. sch.)		1937 = 100	
1946	I	10·6	3·4	—	—
	II	17·7	16·2	—	—
	III	31·5	24·1	—	—
	IV	23·8	29·4	11	13
1947	I	52·7	32·3	15	16
	II	95·3	61·6	25	26
	III	115·6	72·0	28	27
	IV	133·5	114·9	32	40
1948	I	181·6	112·1	37	36
	II	198·5	156·4	44	50
	III	225·3	168·5	52	56
	IV	261·9	221·5	56	65
1949	I	308·0	248·3	65	68
	II	357·2	279·5	75	73
	III	369·7	243·5	80	66
	IV	460·6	304·8	87	75

* Imports include all commercial imports and a part of the relief imports (in particular, all the coal imports and the goods imported under the 'drawing rights' scheme in the E.R.P. programme).

Appendix II

Publications

A. Periodicals

There exists in Austria a great variety of periodicals containing current economic information and articles. Here, however, only those periodicals are mentioned which deal regularly with major economic issues and whose view-point can be regarded as significant.

Factual information (statistics and articles) can be found above all in the following publications:

Statistische Nachrichten. Monthly journal of the Central Statistical Office. Vienna.

Monatsberichte des Österreichischen Instituts für Wirtschaftsforschung. Vienna.

Mitteilungen des Direktoriums der Österreichischen Nationalbank. Monthly journal of the Austrian Central Bank. Vienna.

Civil Affairs Austria. Report of the United States High Commissioner in Austria with a separate Statistical Annex.

Important articles on economic events reflecting various opinions can be found in the following periodicals:

Zeitschrift für Nationaloekonomie. A periodical dealing mainly with theoretical problems but also with questions of economic policy. Appears at irregular intervals. Edited by Professors H. Mayer and A. Mahr. (Publisher: Julius Springer, Vienna.)

Der österreichische Volkswirt. Independent economic journal. Vienna.

Die Industrie. Published by the Association of Austrian Industrialists. Vienna.

Arbeit und Wirtschaft. Published by the Council of Trade Unions and the Chamber of Labour. Vienna.

Monatsberichte and *Wirtschaftsberichte* of the Creditanstalt-Bankverein, the biggest commercial bank. Vienna.

Die Presse. A conservative daily paper whose weekly edition usually carries important economic articles. Vienna.

Die Zukunft. Socialist monthly. Socialist Party. Vienna.

Weg und Ziel. Communist monthly. Communist Party. Vienna.

Berichte und Informationen. A fortnightly periodical of the extreme right wing. Austrian Research Institute for Economics and Politics. Salzburg.

B. Books

A large number of books have been published since the end of the war which deal with the problems of specific industries or other special questions. These have been omitted from the list below and only books dealing with larger spheres of the economy have been included.

Ausch, Karl. *Die neue Wirtschaft im neuen Österreich.* London, 1945.

Bayer, Hans. *Die Zukunft der österreichischen Volkswirtschaft.* Innsbruck, 1947.

Bundespressedienst. *Vier Jahre Wiederaufbau.* Vienna, 1949.

Economic Co-operation Administration. *Austria, Country Study : European Recovery Program.* Washington, 1949.

APPENDICES

Granigg, Bartel. *Die Bodenschätze Österreichs und ihre wirtschaftliche Bedeutung.* Vienna, 1947.

Hertz, Frederick. *The Economic Problem of the Danubian States.* London, 1947.

Hudeczek, Carl. *Die österreichische Volkswirtschaft und ihr Wiederaufbau.* Vienna, 1946.

Lang, C. L. *Destin de l'Autriche.* Paris, 1945.

Macartney, C. A. *Problems of the Danube Basin.* London, 1944.

Mayer, Hans, ed., *Hundert Jahre österreichischer Wirtschaftsentwicklung 1848-1948.* Vienna, 1949.

Nemschak, Franz. *Hauptprobleme der österreichischen Wirtschaftspolitik.* Vienna, 1947.

—— *Die österreichische Volkswirtschaft. I. Die Grundlagen; II. Die Struktur.* Vienna, 1948.

Österreichisches Institut für Wirtschaftsforschung. *Gesamtschau der österreichischen Wirtschaft im Jahre 1947.* Vienna, 1948.

Rauscher, Franz. *Die Verstaatlichung in Österreich.* Vienna, 1949.

Robetschek, Ernst. *Die Wirtschaftssubstanz Österreichs.* Vienna, 1949.

Tautscher, Anton, and Kübler, Ernst. *Die Lebensfähigkeit Österreichs; Untersuchungen und Ausblick.* Vienna-Graz, 1946.

Vereinigung österreichischer Industrieller. *Das Kernproblem der österreichischen Wirtschaft.* Vienna, 1947.

Wirtschaftspolitische Kommission beim Zentralkomitee der Kommunistischen Partei Österreichs. *Der Weg zum Wohlstand; ein österreichischer Wirtschaftsplan.* Vienna, 1948.

INDEX

81

INDEX

82

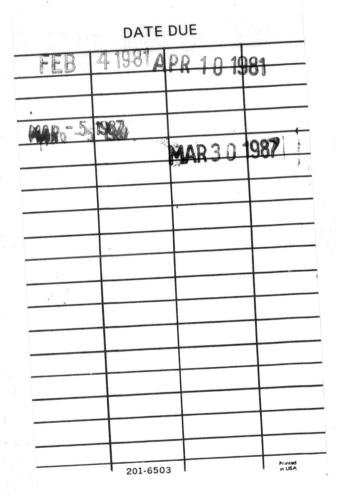